Spanish
Picture Dictionary

Jeremy Munday • Dilys Brown

Contents

Introduction

A picture dictionary is ideal for introducing children to a new language even before they have started formal lessons in the subject at school. Children can 'read' picture dictionaries without knowing how to read or write any words at all – either in their own language or in English. Children can also compare their experience of the world with the wider world illustrated in the dictionary.

The Macmillan Spanish Picture Dictionary contains about 700 words chosen for their high frequency value and their appeal to young learners of Spanish.

▶ Children will recognise objects and activities they are familiar with in their own language.

▶ They will make exciting discoveries on their own and will want to ask about things they are unfamiliar with.

▶ They will start using the words in Spanish and enjoy the experience of new names for things they already know in their own language.

▶ They will acquire a firm foundation of Spanish vocabulary even before they start learning Spanish at school.

▶ At school, the dictionary can be used as an exciting way of teaching new vocabulary and dictionary skills to beginners' classes.

The Macmillan Spanish Picture Dictionary introduces children to Spanish words systematically and meaningfully. There are two sections:

● an alphabetical wordlist containing almost all the words included in the dictionary;

● theme pages, which introduce related words in context. More than two-thirds of the words listed in the dictionary are also illustrated in the theme pages.

Teachers and parents can help children by involving them in activities designed to introduce them to Spanish and to extend their knowledge of it at a manageable pace. Detailed teaching notes and suggestions for practice activities, including tasks for children who have not yet started Spanish lessons as well as activities for children who have already begun to develop a vocabulary in Spanish, begin on page 8.

Map

Spanish is one of the main languages of the world. It is spoken as a main language by around 320 million people in over 20 different countries. The map below shows countries around the Caribbean where Spanish is an official language.

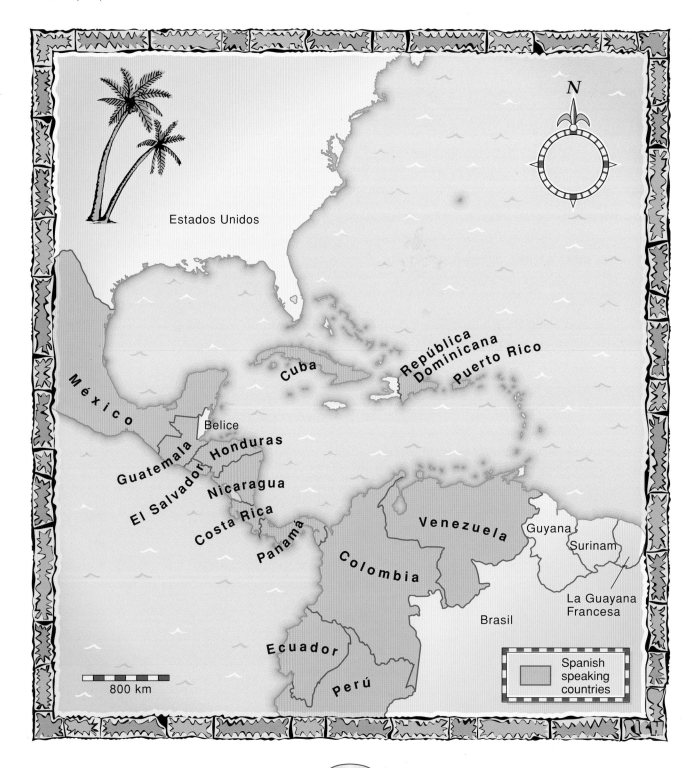

Estados Unidos

México

Cuba

República Dominicana

Puerto Rico

Belice

Guatemala

Honduras

El Salvador

Nicaragua

Costa Rica

Panamá

Colombia

Venezuela

Guyana

Surinam

La Guayana Francesa

Brasil

Ecuador

Perú

800 km

Spanish speaking countries

N

Pronunciation

To learn to pronounce Spanish you really need the help of a teacher or someone else who already knows Spanish, or a tape. For this reason, the tips below point out just some of the sounds that are most likely to be difficult for a learner of Spanish whose mother tongue is English.

In Spanish all the letters are pronounced except the letter *h*.

C is pronounced as in the English word 'car' except when it is followed by *i* or *e*. In the Americas *ci* and *ce* are pronounced like *si* and *se*. For example, *cielo, cerro*.

Ch is always pronounced as in the English 'church'. For example, *champú*.

A *d* between two vowels is pronounced like the English 'th' in a word such as 'this'. For example, *cerrado*.

A *g* is pronounced more or less like the English 'g' in 'garden' (for example, *gato*) except when it is followed by *e* or *i*. Then it is pronounced like the Spanish *j* (see below). For example, *gente*.

An *h* is not pronounced. For example, *hombre*.

A *j* is pronounced a little bit like a strong English 'h' at the back of the throat. For example, *jabón*.

An *ll* is pronounced a little bit like an English 'y' in 'yet'. For example, *lluvia*.

An *ñ* is pronounced a little bit like the 'ni' in 'onion'. For example, *España*.

Qu is pronounced like the English 'k' in 'kilometre'. For example, *queso*.

RR is a strong rolling sound. For example, *pizarra*.

The Spanish letter *v* is pronounced more or less the same as the Spanish letter *b*. It is like a soft English 'b'. Try saying a 'b' as in 'ball', with your lips only lightly touching. For example, *vaca*.

Z in the Americas is always pronounced like the 's' in 'salt'. For example, *zoo*.

Word stress

If a word ends in a vowel, *s* or *n* it will be stressed on the second to last syllable. For example, **ca**rro, Ca**ri**be, aero**mo**za. If a word ends in any other letter it will be stressed on the last syllable. For example, alfi**ler**, a**zul**, escri**bir**.

If a word does not follow these rules then an accent mark shows where to stress it. For example, a**zú**car, bo**tón**, hura**cán**.

Grammar points

'El' or 'la' ?

Most of the words in this book are things, people or animals (for example, *aeropuerto, camisa, médico, elefante*.) These words are called **nouns**. In English we can use 'the' with all these nouns. However in Spanish, nouns are either what is called **masculine** ('male') or **feminine** ('female') and these have different words for 'the'. These words for 'the' are *el* (masculine) and *la* (feminine). Below are some examples of people and animals that are masculine and feminine:

masculine	feminine
el niño (boy)	*la niña* (girl)
el hermano (brother)	*la hermana* (sister)
el alumno (male pupil)	*la alumna* (female pupil)
el gato (male cat)	*la gata* (female cat)

As you can see, masculine words often end in *o* and feminine words often end in *a*. This is a very useful rule but it does not work in every case. For example, the word *artista* (artist) can be masculine (*el artista*, for a man) or feminine (*la artista*, for a woman).

What's more, in Spanish every noun is either masculine or feminine even when it is a thing and not a person or animal. Some examples are below:

masculine	feminine
el vestido (the dress)	*la camisa* (the shirt)
el vaso (the glass)	*la cuchara* (the spoon)
el tenedor (the fork)	*la flor* (the flower)

Because there is no way of telling if a word is going to be masculine or feminine, it is very important to learn both the word and the *el* or the *la* that goes with it. So, for example, don't just learn *vestido*, learn *el vestido*. That is why all the nouns in this dictionary have *el* or *la* in front of them.

What if there is more than one?

If a noun is **plural** (that is, if there is more than one of a thing, person or animal), then the word for 'the' is different. You need to use *los* for masculine words and *las* for feminine words. And you usually need to put an *s* on the end of the noun. For example:

masculine	feminine
los niños	*las niñas*
los hermanos	*las hermanas*
los vasos	*las cucharas.*

For words that end in a consonant, you usually need to put *es* on the end in the plural. For example:

los tenedores	*las flores*

How do you say 'a' and 'an' ?

Once you've learnt if a word is *el* (masculine) or *la* (feminine), then learning how to say 'a' and 'an' is easy. If it is a masculine word you use *un*, and if it is a feminine word you use *una*. For example:

masculine	feminine
un niño	*una niña*
un hermano	*una hermana*
un alumno	*una alumna*
un gato	*una gata*
un vestido	*una camisa*
un tenedor	*una flor*

Do any words not follow these rules?

There are just a few exceptions to the rules. Feminine words beginning with a stressed *a* or *ha* use the word *el* for 'the' and *un* for 'a'. This is to make pronunciation easier. In this dictionary the only words like this are *agua, águila* and *hacha*.

Describing words

On the colours page (page 82) and the descriptions page (page 84), you will see a lot of words that are used to describe things. For example, *rojo* (red), *amarillo* (yellow), *alto* (tall). The endings of these kinds of describing words, which are called **adjectives**, also change depending on whether they are used with masculine or feminine nouns. And they usually go after the word they describe. Below are some examples:

masculine	feminine
el *vestid**o** amarill**o***	**la** *camis**a** roj**a***
(the yellow dress)	(the red shirt)
los *vestid**os** amarill**os***	**las** *camis**as** roj**as***
(the yellow dresses)	(the red shirts)
el *alumn**o** alt**o***	**la** *niñ**a** alt**a***
(the tall pupil)	(the tall girl)
los *alumn**os** alt**os***	**las** *niñ**as** alt**as***
(the tall pupils)	(the tall girls)

Look at how sounds of the endings of words that are used together very often are the same. Notice the *os* in **los** *vestid**os** amarill**os***, and the *as* in **las** *niñ**as** alt**as***. You can 'hear' the rhymes in the words.

Search terms!

This is a short quiz to see if you can find different types of information in this *Picture Dictionary*. In each case, choose from one of three possible answers.

1 On which page can you find the names of countries where Spanish is the official language? a) 4, b) 5, c) 6.

2 How many different Spanish words for 'the' are there? a) 2, b) 3, c) 4.

3 Which word would you use for 'a' with the Spanish word *familia*? a) *un*, b) *una*, c) *unas*.

4 Which letter in the Spanish alphabet comes between *n* and *o* ? a) *q*, b) *ñ*, c) *p*.

5 Which page contains a list of numbers? a) 6, b) 44, c) 81.

6 On which page can you find words to describe people? a) 63, b) 84, c) 85.

7 What does the Spanish word *cabeza* mean? a) head, b) hair, c) face.

8 On which pages does the Spanish word *ligero* appear? a) 52, b) 52 and 85, c) 52, 85, 98 and 114.

9 If you want to check what *pluma fuente* means, which pages should you look at? a) 65 and 112, b) 65 and 107, c) 65 and 110.

10 If you want to find out how to say 'swimming pool' in Mexico, which page can you look at? a) 64, b) 70, c) 115.
Solutions on page 117.

Teaching notes

Using the dictionary

As discussed in the introduction, young learners of Spanish will enjoy using their *Macmillan Spanish Picture Dictionary*, looking at the pictures, describing what they can see and learning new words in Spanish.

Encourage the children to read their book and look at the pictures, even before they start learning Spanish at school. Prompt them to talk about their favourite illustrations and words, discuss the pictures and meanings and say why they like them.

Below you will find suggestions for teaching and practice activities, but first here are a few notes about the organisation of the dictionary.

The pronunciation page

To learn to pronounce Spanish the help of a teacher or other Spanish speaker is required. The descriptions on this page just highlight some of the more difficult sounds for a beginner. It is important for the teacher of the class to stress and practise pronunciation with the pupils from an early stage. The pronunciation described is a general Spanish American one.

The grammar page

Because most of the words in the dictionary are nouns or adjectives, the grammar pages confine themselves to a description of gender, definite and indefinite articles and adjectival inflections. A few essential grammatical terms are introduced (for example, 'masculine', 'feminine').

The *Search terms!* page

This page is a short quiz which helps introduce some basic dictionary skills to the children. By doing the quiz the children can learn about alphabetical organisation (the extra letter *ñ*) and whereabouts in the dictionary different information is located (the numbers page, where to check the sense of a Spanish word, where to look up an English word, etc). Encourage the children to return to the page later for help in finding other information. Get them to make up their own 'Search terms!' quiz and to test out their class mates.

The alphabetical section

All words in the dictionary are illustrated in the main alphabetical section except for numbers, dates, colours and most of the words in the **Descriptions** spread. These words are deliberately excluded because they are difficult to illustrate meaningfully out of context. There are some common words which have important regional variations. These variations are indicated by (Méx) for words used in Mexico, (Venz) for Venezuela, (PtRi) for Puerto Rico, (RD) for the Dominican Republic, and (Cuba) for Cuba. For example, 'banana' is *la banana*, *el cambur* (Venz), *el guineo* (PtRi), *el plátano* (Méx), where the Spanish *la banana* is the general word and the other three are regional variations.

The theme pages

Some of the theme pages are single-page illustrations; some are double-page spreads.

The main words related to each theme page topic area are listed on the page, with a number against each. The items in the picture have a small circle on or next to them which contains the corresponding number. This is designed to allow the teacher to carry out matching activities (see **Using the theme pages**, page 12).

The Wordlists

The Wordlists include a complete list of all the words illustrated in the alphabetical section of the dictionary and all the main words illustrated on the theme pages. There are two Wordlists: the Spanish–English Wordlist is designed to enable children to be absolutely sure that they have understood the sense of a Spanish word illustrated in the text. The English–Spanish Wordlist is designed so that the children can search for the translation of an English word they might need but which they can't remember at the time.

In all cases the English translation equivalent given is the most frequent equivalent for the Spanish word, but it should always be checked by referring back to the picture of the item in the dictionary. In this way, the children are being introduced to the basics of monolingual and bilingual dictionaries. The Wordlists function as a basic bilingual dictionary, but the importance is being stressed of using a monolingual reference and a picture that represents a real-world situation.

The alphabet

When you teach the Spanish alphabet, the children will need to know that Spanish used to use (and in some cases still does use) the letters *ch*, *ll* and *ñ* in addition to the 26 letters used in English. Note, however, that as far as alphabetical order is concerned, we have followed the current trend in Spanish dictionaries and included words beginning with *ch* and *ll* under the letters *c* and *l*. For example, *champú* comes after *cesta* and before *cielo*. *Ñ* is still treated as a separate letter.

It is useful for the children to see and start learning the alphabet right from the beginning.

1 Make an alphabet frieze for the classroom:
   Aa Bb Cc Dd Ee Ff Gg Hh Ii Jj Kk Ll Mm Nn
   Ññ Oo Pp Qq Rr Ss Tt Uu Vv Ww Xx Yy Zz.
2 Chant the alphabet daily, pointing to the letters.
3 Divide the class into two groups and get the groups to chant the alphabet, each group chanting alternate letters.
4 Point to individual children and get each one to say the next letter in the alphabet.
5 If you use several colours to make the frieze, when the children have learnt the alphabet, you can ask them to say all the blue letters, the red letters and so on.
6 If you have a large class, give letter cards to 27 children (or 54 if you use capital letters and small letters) and get them to stand in alphabetical order.
7 Point to letters in the alphabet frieze and get the children to find a word beginning with that letter in their dictionary.

Numbers and colours

Numbers and colours should be taught very early. The dictionary is ideal for introducing these key vocabulary areas. Once numbers and colours are known, they can be incorporated into many types of practice activity. See below.

Note: Although only zero and numbers 1–21 are formally presented on page 81, the calendar gives the numbers to 31 and page numbers in the dictionary can be used to teach higher numbers. These will be useful for introducing dictionary and reference skills later on. Colours are presented on page 82.

Here are some simple practice activities you can use to teach numbers and colours.

Number activities

1 Point to individual children and get each child to say the next number in a sequence. Begin with short sequences, e.g. 1–5, 6–10 etc., then gradually move to longer sequences, e.g. 1–10, 1–20.

2 Once the numbers 1–20 have been introduced, encourage the children – as a group then individually – to say the whole sequence.
3 Say two or three consecutive numbers, e.g. 4, 5, 6, and get the class, then individual pupils, to continue the sequence.
4 Ask the children to stand in groups of *seis*, *siete*, *diez* etc.
5 Ask the children to count the boys, the windows, pupils with green shoes, etc.
6 Then introduce higher numbers, say 20–30, 30–40, and so on, as with **1** and **2** above.
7 Tell the children to find e.g. *página siete*, *página diecinueve*, *página tres* in their dictionary as quickly as possible.
8 Ask one child to pick a number between 1 and 20, or 21 and 40 etc. Ask the other children to guess what that number is. One child at a time calls out a number in Spanish until they guess the number thought of by the first child. Do this in groups.
9 Play a game of bingo with the children. The children write down six numbers between 1 and 40. Call out one number at a time. The children cross off each number they have written down when they hear you say it. When a child has crossed out all of his/her numbers, he or she calls out *¡Bingo!* and then reads out the six numbers.

Colour activities

1 Say a colour. Ask the class to point to something yellow, blue, red etc.
2 Say a colour. Ask the individual children to point or touch something red, black, orange etc.
3 Ask the children what their favourite colour is. Get them to stand in 'favourite colour' groups.
4 Ask the children with the same colour of socks, sweater, pen, etc. to stand in groups.
5 As the children become more aware of the gender differences of nouns and the adjectival inflections in Spanish, try the second activity above using the inflection of the adjective.
   For example, ask individual children to point to something that is *amarilla* (rather than *amarillo*).

Using the classroom to teach numbers and colours

Make full use of the classroom to familiarise the children with numbers and colours.

Prepare colour cards, number cards and word cards.

Teach the names of objects in the classroom (see **En la escuela**, page 83).

Do counting and identifying activities using objects in the classroom – every day if possible.

Here are some ideas:

1 First attach appropriate colour cards to different objects in the classroom.

2 Say the colour and get the class and/or individual children to name the object.

3 Name the object and get the class and/or individual children to say the colour, with the correct adjectival inflection.

4 Ask individual children to say the colours and other children to name the objects.

5 Ask individual children to name the objects and other children to say the colours.

Note: You can carry out all these activities using number cards instead of colour cards. Use different sets of numbers each time!

6 Give 6–10 children a number or a colour card and ask them to attach the card to an object they know. After all the children have attached their number/colour cards, ask each one to say the number/colour and the name of the object.

7 Ask 6–10 children to attach a card to something they *don't* know and would like to know the name for!

Using the *En la escuela* theme page

1 Once the children are familiar with most classroom vocabulary, tell the class to look at the **En la escuela** theme page, page 83.
Divide the class into pairs.
In turns, they point and say what they can see in the classroom picture, or ask each other questions and give each other instructions.
Introduce different patterns, e.g.

Veo _____.
Es un/una _____.
Hay un/una _____.
¿Ves el/la _____?

2 Distribute word cards to individual pupils. In turns, pupils with word cards attach their card to the appropriate object.

3 Suggest to the children that they try this activity at home. They can attach cards or Post-It notes with the Spanish word to the appropriate object in their bedrooms, or in the rest of the house. But they should ask their parents' permission first!

Using the alphabetical section of the dictionary

1 **¡Busquen los/las_____!**
This is a pronunciation-practising activity suitable for those just beginning to learn Spanish.
● Ask the children to look for words in one group, e.g. animals, fruit, toys, vehicles, in the alphabetical section of the dictionary.

● First, let the children work at their own pace. They can work by themselves or in pairs to look for appropriate pictures.

● Next, starting at the beginning of the alphabetical section, instruct them to turn the pages all at the same time and put their hands up if they can see an animal, a fruit, a toy etc.

● As the children find words, hold up the dictionary and teach the words, building up the children's vocabulary, bit by bit.

● Return to this activity several times, noting how many words the children have remembered each time.

Note: For several groups of words, there is also a theme page in the dictionary. After several words in the group are known, turn to the appropriate theme page and let the children work in pairs or small groups to say the words they know.

2 **¿Cómo se llama el/la _____?**
This is a team game for revising word groups.
● Divide the class into two teams.
● Tell the class what kind of item they have to look for, e.g. vegetables, animals, food, things you find in the kitchen, parts of the body.
● Tell the class which page to look at, or write the page number on the board.
● In turns, team members point to and name an item.
● If a child gets an answer wrong, or fails to spot a word on a page, members of the other team can answer and gain a point for the team if they answer correctly.
● The team with the highest score wins.

3 **¡Busquen el/la_____!**
This is a pair or group activity for revising word groups.
● Once the children know a fair number of the words in a word group, they can be given a set time, e.g. three minutes, to find all the words they can.
● Tell the children to mark the relevant pages in the dictionary with a small slip of paper.
● Ask each pair/group how many words they have found.
● The pair/group with the largest number – or the smallest number – say the words they found.
● Other pairs/groups then say any other words they found.

4 **¿Cuántos/cuántas _____ pueden encontrar?**
This is a variation on Activity 3.
● Ask the children to find words in a group, e.g. animals, toys, things to eat, green objects. The number will vary depending on the knowledge of the children. Children just

starting to learn Spanish should not have to find more than four or five pictures.

- The children look through the alphabetical section of the dictionary until they find appropriate pictures. They write down the words they find and the page numbers next to them.
- Give as many children as possible the chance to report what they have found.
- The children can then check against the theme pages to see if there are any words they have missed.

5 Pistas – mi _____ favorito/favorita

This is an activity for slightly more advanced pupils.

- Four or five pupils choose a favourite thing and give clues, e.g.

  Mi animal favorito es pequeño. Es gris. Está en la página 104.

  Mi juguete favorito: Es redondo. Es blanco y negro. Está en la página 90.

  Mi vegetal favorito: Es naranja y verde. Es largo. Está en la página 98.

- The rest of the class listen and try to name the items. They can try to guess the answer after each clue, or write down the answers after listening to all the clues and referring to the dictionary.

6 ¿Pueden encontrar la palabra_____?

This is an activity to practise dictionary and comprehension skills.

- The teacher asks: '*¿Pueden encontrar la palabra_____?*'
- The class try to find the item as quickly as possible.
- The first pupil to identify the correct page and picture picks the next word and asks the question.
- Continue until about ten children have asked and answered questions.

7 Sé decir

This is a revision activity to improve pronunciation (and spelling).

- Divide the class into two teams.
- Everyone looks at a two-page spread from the alphabet section where all the words are known.
- In turns, children from each team choose a word to say (and spell, if they know how).
- If a child makes a mistake in the pronunciation (or spelling), a member of the other team gets the chance to say the word.
- Continue until all the pictures on the spread have been identified.
- Repeat with one other spread if the children are still involved and interested in the activity.
- The team with the highest score wins.

8 ¿Qué es?

This is a fluency and reference practice activity similar to Activity 5.

- Children choose their own page or spread and give clues to their chosen word and picture. In the early stages of learning the clues can be given in English:

  My word is on page 105. It's a short word. The picture is orange and black. It's an animal.

- After every clue the children try to guess the word.
- The first child to guess correctly gives clues to a different word on a different page.
- As the children progress, the clues can be given in Spanish:

  Mi palabra está en la página 105. Es una palabra corta. El dibujo es naranja y negro. Es un animal.

9 ¡Búsquenlo!/¡Búsquenla!

This is a page-turning activity for young learners.

- Children leaf through the dictionary to find whatever they are asked to, e.g.

  Find a toy you like playing with.
  Find a very big animal.
  Find something you like to eat.
  Find a green thing.
  Find something you see in a living room.
  Find a fruit.
  Find a good job.
  Find something you sometimes eat for breakfast.
  Find a birthday present for _____.

- Two or three children say what they have found after every search.
- As the children progress, the simple questions can soon be asked in Spanish.

10 Memoria

This is a variation of Kim's Game, where children have to remember all the items on a tray.

- All the children look at a page or a two-page spread in the alphabet section for two minutes and try to memorise every word on the page.

Note: Choose a spread where all the words are known.
* If all the words begin with the same initial letter, you can do the follow-up activity described below.

- After two minutes, the children close their books.
- They put their hands up when they are ready to say what they can remember.
- Ask one child to say all the words he or she can remember.
- Ask one child to add any missing words.

* Further practice: do pronunciation practice of all the words beginning with the same initial letter, particularly those where there are differences. For instance, if the initial letter is *c*, then each child has

to try to pronounce one of the words, *carro*, *cerdo*, *chico*, *cielo*, *cocina*, etc.

11 Alphabetical order

This is an activity based on Activity 10 above, but extended to include a writing and ordering activity.

- All the children look at a page or a two-page spread in the alphabetic section for two minutes.
- They close their books.
- The children write down all the words they can remember.
- They put their hands up when they are ready.
- One child reads out his or her list.
- Write the words on the board as they are read.
- Ask other children to add any missing words.
- The children add any missing words.
- The children add any missing words to their list and correct any spelling mistakes.
- Tell the children to write the words in the correct alphabetical order.
- You can then ask one child to read out the alphabetical list and write it on the board, and/or all the children can check their lists by looking at the appropriate page in the dictionary.

Note: It may be helpful if you write on the board initially, but later encourage the children to use their dictionary as a reference source.

12 Conozco (un vegetal) que empieza con _____.

This is a reference practice activity for children familiar with the pronunciation of the Spanish alphabet.

- One child chooses an animal/a fruit/a vegetable/a job/a vehicle and says:

    Conozco una fruta que empieza con A (or B, C, etc). *¿ Qué es ?*

    ¿ En qué página está ?

- The rest of the class look for the word and put their hands up when they find it.
- One child says:

    Es un aguacate. Está en la página 17.

- If the answer is correct, the child answering chooses a word.
- If the answer is wrong, another child guesses until the correct answer is found.

    Es un albaricoque. Está en la página 17.

- Continue until five or six children have said their chosen word.

13 ¿Con qué letra empieza la palabra (jirafa)?

This is a reference practice activity for children becoming familiar with the Spanish alphabet.

- Choose a word group, e.g. clothes, furniture.
- Ask the class to choose a word in the group and write it down.
- One child asks the questions:

    ¿Con qué letra empieza la palabra jirafa/mesa/silla/bufanda/naranja?

¿En qué página está?

- Another answers, and asks the next question if their answer is correct.
- Continue until five or six children have had a turn.

14 Tareas

This is a reference practice activity for more advanced children.

- Make two packs of cards. One pack contains *palabras*, words the children have learned. The other pack contains *tareas*, tasks the children must do (e.g. 'spell the word', 'spell the word backwards', 'give another word on the same theme page', 'give a word that means the opposite to it').
- Divide the class into two teams, A and B.
- Pick the first card from the *palabras* pack, and the first card from the *tareas* pack. Team A then has to perform that task with that word. If they do it correctly they get a point. If they don't, Team B has the chance of answering for a bonus point.
- Pick the second card from the *palabras* pack, and the second card from the *tareas* pack. Team B then has to perform that task with that word. Continue until one team reaches ten points.
- This game can also be played in pairs or small groups.

Using the theme pages

General notes

On most of the theme pages (apart from **La familia** and **Descripciones**, where the different items are individually captioned), selected words related to the topics are listed in alphabetical order and numbered in sequence. On or next to each of these objects, people, activities or places in the picture there is a small circle containing the corresponding number. The circles act as a guide, to help the children identify the items in the picture, learn their names and recognise the shape of the words.

The Wordlists on the theme pages can also be used for dictionary practice.

Ask the class to look for the listed words in the alphabetical section of the dictionary and say or write the corresponding page number for each word.

In addition to the words listed, other words are illustrated on the theme pages. These may already be known or, if not, they can be taught. The children should be encouraged to learn as many as possible. They can make their own extended wordlists to accompany the theme pages.

With every theme page:

- Encourage the children to describe what they can see.
- Encourage them to ask for words they don't know.
- Prompt them to answer questions and offer their own comments and observations, e.g.

> Veo un/una/dos_____ .
> Hay un/una_____ verde.
> Tengo un/una_____ .
> Me gusta el/la_____ .
> ¿Qué quiere decir '_____ '?
> ¿Cómo se dice '_____ ' en español?
> ¿Qué se puede ver en el campo/en la calle/en el salón?
> ¿Qué ropa lleva el niño de la izquierda?
> ¿Qué comida/juguetes/juegos ves?
> ¿Tú tienes algunas de estas cosas?

- The children can tell memory stories, using the pictures as prompts, e.g.

> The first child says, 'Ayer hice las compras. Compré una manzana.'
> The second child repeats what the first child says and adds an item, e.g. 'Ayer hice las compras. Compré una manzana y una banana.'
> The third child repeats what the second child says and adds another item, e.g. 'Ayer hice las compras. Compré una manzana, una banana y una pera.'
> A child drops out if he or she cannot remember the whole list. Continue until there is only one child left or until all the words have been exhausted.

- Encourage the children to work in pairs or small groups, helping each other to build up vocabulary, and playing these memory games. Two, three or four heads are usually better than one!

A special note about Descripciones, pages 84–85
As with the words in the **Números y fechas** page, most of the words in **Descripciones** do not appear in the alphabetical list because they are difficult to illustrate in isolation. They will be understood and learned much more easily when shown in context and in relation to other words.

You are advised not to try to teach all the word group at once. Choose a few at a time, e.g. words to describe how people look; words to describe how people feel; prepositions describing where things are; shapes.

You may want to add a few extra words to help the children express themselves.

Here are a few ideas for using the individual theme pages. You will be able to adapt ideas given for one particular spread for use with several others.

Los números y las fechas (page 81)
See the introductory section of the Teaching Notes, page 9.

1 Write the date on the board every day.
2 Teach the children the days of the week and the months of the year gradually.
3 Introduce time once numbers 1–12 are known, with the expressions, ¿Qué hora es? Es la una/son las dos, etc.

Los colores y la ropa (page 82)
1 Teach the names of the items of clothing.
2 Get the children to describe the colours of the clothes on page 82.
3 Let them describe their own and each other's clothes.
4 Ask the children what they wear to parties, or when they come to school, when they are playing games and so on, e.g. Cuando juego al fútbol, llevo unas botas marrones, un short blanco y una camiseta verde.

En la escuela (page 83)
See the introductory section of the Teaching Notes on page 9 for ideas on exploiting this page.

Las descripciones (pages 84–85)
The following activity can be used with more advanced pupils in conjunction with other theme pages to practise both vocabulary and prepositions.

1 Teach the children the prepositions (dentro, al lado de, etc.).
2 One of the children imagines where a particular animal or object is hidden in the classroom. He or she writes down the name of the object and where it is hidden.
3 The other children ask questions to find out where it is and what it is, for example, ¿Está en la mesa del profesor? The first child can only answer sí or no. The first person who discovers where the object is and what it is, calls it out.

Los trabajos (page 86)
1 Teach the words.
2 Teach the difference between the masculine and feminine endings, e.g. profesor, profesora and the fact that the definite article is often not used with jobs.
3 Ask the children to say what they would like to be, e.g. Quiero ser bombero.
4 Ask individual children to come and mime one of the jobs. The rest of the class have to guess which job it is.
Note: You can also get the children to write down the jobs they have guessed, then ask them to correct any spelling mistakes by checking in the dictionary. They can then put the words into alphabetical order.
5 Ask a few children to make noises related to the jobs illustrated – the class have to guess which job it is!

6 Play *Memoria* (see Activity 10, page 11). The children look at the page for two minutes, then close their books and try to remember every job illustrated.

7 Play *¡Busquen el trabajo!*. On the board, write a dash for every letter in the job name. The children guess letters and gradually the word is completed, e.g. – – – – – – – = *cartero*.
The child who guesses first chooses another job.

8 Ask the children if they can think of other jobs which are not listed on this page, e.g. clown, taxi driver etc., and get them to complete a wordlist of jobs.

La familia (page 87)

1 Teach the words.

2 Tell the children to draw members of their own family and label their drawing.

3 Ask the children to say how many brothers and sisters they've got.

4 Encourage them to name their brothers and sisters:
Tengo una hermana mayor que se llama
_____ . *Mis hermanos se llaman* _____ y
_____ .

5 Find out if anyone in the class is a twin, or knows any twins. (Teach the words *gemelos, gemelas, mellizos, mellizas*.)

En casa (pages 88–89)

1 Teach the words relevant to each room in turn.

2 Play *Memoria* (see Activity 10, page 11) The children look at one of the rooms for two minutes, close their books then try to remember things in the room.

3 Play *¡Búsquenlo/la!* (see Activity 9, page 11). On the board, write a dash for every letter in the name of an object. The children guess letters and gradually the word is completed, e.g. *En la cocina* – – – – = *vaso*.
The child who guesses first chooses another object.

4 Let the children describe each room in their home and say what is in it.

5 When all the rooms are learnt, say an object and let the children say which room you find it in. They should then point to the object named, e.g. *jabón* = *el cuarto de baño*; *una sábana* = *la recámara*.
Note: Some words will belong in more than one room, e.g. *una mata*. Accept any correct answer!

6 Get the children to draw their own bedroom and talk about their drawing.

El recreo (pages 90–91)

1 Teach the words.

2 Ask the children to describe the objects.

3 Say words very quickly and get the children to point to the objects.

4 Let the children say what they like doing or playing with.

5 Play *Memoria* (see Activity 10, page 11).

6 Play *¡Búsquenlo/la!* (see Activity 9, page 11).

7 Ask the children to say what they would like as a present.

8 Write an initial letter on the board and ask the children to say all the words they can see beginning with that letter, e.g. *b, c, p*.

En el campo (pages 92–93)

1 Teach the words and practise them in groups, e.g. animals, scenery, farm words etc.

2 Do listing and matching exercises with animals: the children list all the farm animals they can see and match them with their young.

3 Ask the children to do a mime related to the animals – the rest of the class have to guess which animal it is!

4 Play *Memoria*. The children look at the page for two minutes, close their books then try to remember every animal/type of scenery/green thing illustrated.

5 Play *¡Búsquenlo/la!* (see Activity 9, page 11). On the board, write a dash for every letter in the name of an object. The children guess letters and gradually the word is completed, e.g. – – – – – – = *granja*.
The child who guesses first chooses another word.

6 Write an initial letter on the board and ask the children to say all the words they can see beginning with that letter, e.g. *b, c, f, r, s*.

7 Play Spanish I-spy. The teacher chooses a word.
Teacher: *Veo veo…*
Class: *¿Qué ves?*
Teacher: *Una cosita.*
Class: *¿Con qué letrita?*
Teacher: *Empieza con la letra* _____ .
The person who guesses the word correctly then chooses another word.

8 Do a picture dictation. Make up a short descriptive text related to the spread. The children draw what you say and then describe their drawing. They can then label it, e.g.
Veo una granja. Hay un árbol en la granja. Hay un pájaro en el árbol y hay dos pájaros en el cielo. Hay un estanque en la granja. Hay seis patos que están nadando en el estanque.

En la playa (pages 94–95)

1 Teach the words.

2 If the children go to the seaside, let them describe what they like doing there.

3 Play *Memoria*.

4 Play *¡Búsquenlo/la!* (see Activity 9, page 11). On the board, write a dash for every letter in the name of an object. The children guess letters and gradually the word is completed, e.g. – – – – – = *arena*.
The child who guesses first chooses another word.

5 Write an initial letter on the board and ask the children to say all the words they can see beginning with that letter, e.g. *c, o, s.*

6 Play *Veo veo* (see **En el campo** above). A child chooses a word and the others guess what it is. The one who guesses correctly then chooses another word.

7 Do a picture dictation. Make up a short descriptive text related to the spread. The children draw what you say and then describe their drawing. They can label it.

En la ciudad (pages 96–97)

1 Teach the words in groups, e.g. vehicles, places.

2 Ask the class to list the types of building next to each other in the street.

3 Other activities described previously:
-¡*Busquen el edificio/el vehículo*! etc.
-*Memoria*
-*Veo veo*
-A picture dictation.

Note: If your class is quite advanced, let one of the children draw a picture and describe it to the others as a picture dictation. Make sure the picture is not too complicated!

En el supermercado (pages 98–99)

1 Get the children to make shopping lists of items they would like to buy from the supermarket.
In pairs they can go shopping:
A: ¿*Dónde está/están* _____ ?
B: (pointing to the food on the page) ¡*Ahí!* or
B: *Está/Están al lado de* _____, *delante de/detrás de* _____, etc.

2 Children can also prepare written or oral lists of vegetables, fruit, containers, favourite food etc.

3 Play the shopping game where everyone who speaks must add an item to the list.
Child A says: *Fui al supermercado y compré manzanas.* Child B says: *Fui al supermercado y compré manzanas y mantequilla.* Child C says: *Fui al supermercado y compré manzanas, mantequilla y caramelos.* Child D says: *Fui al supermercado y compré manzanas, mantequilla, caramelos y zanahorias* (etc.).

4 Play *Memoria*.

5 Other activities described previously.

En el hospital (pages 100–101)

1 Teach the parts of the body first.

2 Play a Simple Simon type game. The teacher says,
Pedro dice '¡Tóquense la cabeza, etc!'
and the children have to touch their head, etc.

3 Teach the other medical words.

4 Play a guessing game to build up a body on the board. Draw a head. The children take turns to say which part of the body comes next. Add each part they say.

5 Get the children to draw and label a body.

6 Other activities described previously.

En el aeropuerto (page 102)

1 Teach the words.

2 Teach the Spanish words for different countries and cities. The map on page 4 can be useful for the Spanish-speaking countries.

3 Ask the children where they have flown to, or where they would like to fly to.

4 Give the children a map of the Americas with some of the cities/nations blanked out. Ask them to write in the names of the cities and nations in Spanish.

5 Other activities such as *Memoria*.

¡Feliz cumpleaños! (page 103)

1 Teach the birthday song:
  ¡Cumpleaños feliz!
  ¡Cumpleaños feliz!
  Te deseamos todos
  ¡Cumpleaños feliz!

2 Check when the children in your class have their birthdays and celebrate them if possible. Ask each child what kind of food they would like at their party.

3 On a birthday, get the rest of the class to make birthday cards for the child celebrating the birthday. They should write the age on it – and draw a present they would like to be able to give the child! (See **El recreo**, pages 90–91).

4 Ask the children to say what they eat at family parties.

5 Other activities described previously.

Los animales (pages 104–105)

1 Teach the words.

2 Ask the children to write the names of all or some of the animals, using their wordlists for reference.

3 Ask them to say or guess what kind of noises some of the animals make.

4 Let one child make a noise while the rest of the class guess what the animal is.

5 Ask them in turns to say what their favourite and least favourite animals are.

6 Ask the children to make two lists: one of animals they have seen and one of animals they haven't seen.

7 Ask the children to write lists of birds, animals, insects etc.

8 The children cover their wordlists. One child says the name of the animal; another child says the number. Vary this by asking children to choose the number of an animal and let the others say the name.

9 Dictate the names of several animals. The class write the words and put number references beside them. They then sort them into alphabetical order.

10 Get the children to draw their favourite animal and write its name. Make posters or a wall display with the pictures.

11 As the children progress, get them to write their own animal poems in Spanish.

Aa

la abeja

abrir

el aeromozo/la aeromoza* (Venz)/la azafata

el abrelatas

el abrigo

la abuela

el abuelo

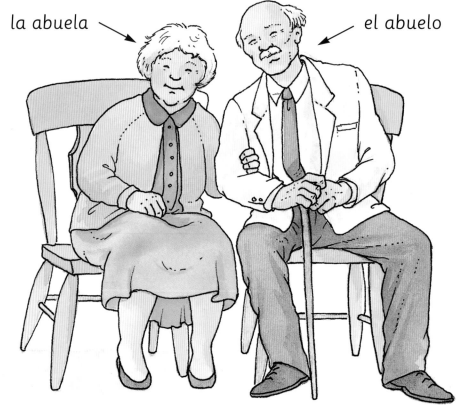

los abuelos

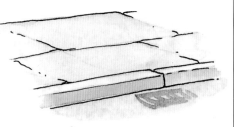

la acera

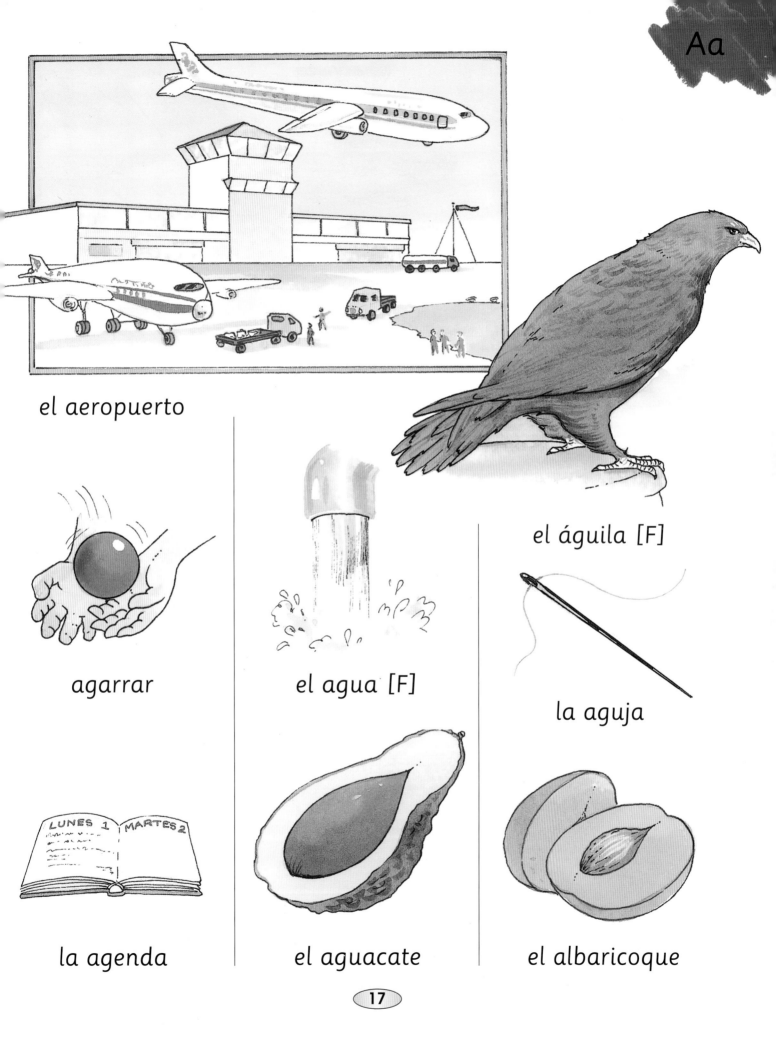

el aeropuerto

el águila [F]

agarrar

el agua [F]

la aguja

la agenda

el aguacate

el albaricoque

Aa

el alfabeto

el alumno/
la alumna*

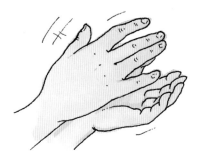

aplaudir

el alfiler

la ambulancia

la araña

la almohada

el anillo

el árbol

la almuerzo

el almuerzo

el animal

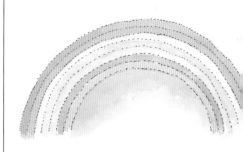

el arco iris

el armario

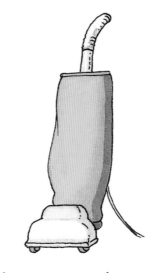

la aspiradora

el/la atleta*

el arroz

el/la artista*

el asiento

el/la astronauta*

el autobús, el camión (Méx), la guagua (Cuba, PtRi)

el avestruz

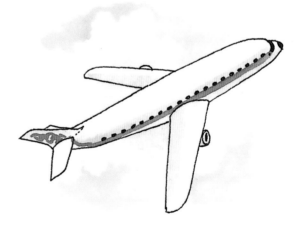

el avión

el azúcar

Bb

bailar

el balcón

la banana,
el cambur(Venz),
el guineo (Cuba, PtRi),
el plátano(Méx)

el bailarín/la
bailarina*

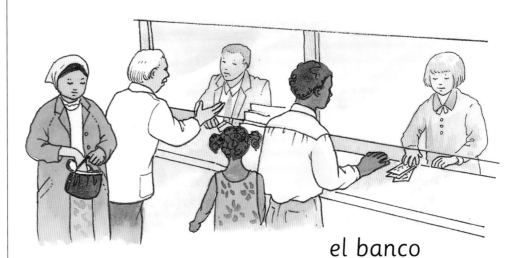

el banco

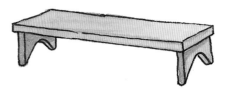

el banco

la bandera

la ballena

Bb

la bañera

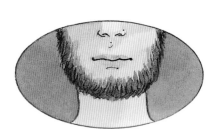

la barba

la barbilla

el barro

el básquetbol,
el baloncesto (Cuba)

el barco de vela

el bastón

el bate

el bebé

beber

22

el béisbol

la biblioteca

la bicicleta

el bigote

el bikini

la blusa

la boca

el bol

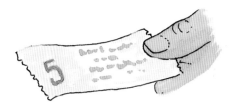

el boleto

el bolígrafo

la bolsa de viaje

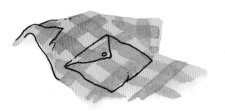

el bolsillo

Bb

la bomba de gasolina

el bote

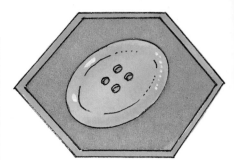

el botón

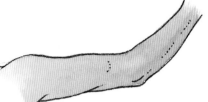

el brazo

el/la bombero*

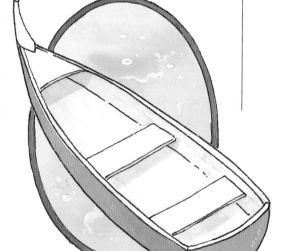

el bote,
la barca

el bronceador

la bufanda

las botas

la botella

el buque

Cc

el caballo

la cabeza

la cabra

la cacerola

el cachorro

el café

el caimán

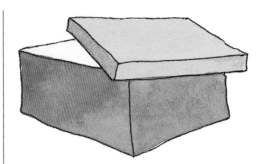

la caja

la caja de acuarelas

el calendario

la calle

el camello

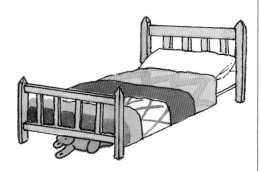

la cama

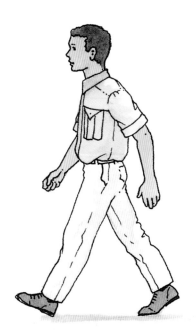

caminar

el camión

la cámara

el camión de
bomberos

el camisón

la camiseta,
la franela (Venz)

la campana

la camioneta

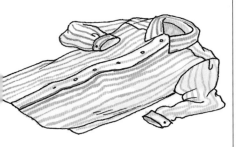

la camisa

el campo

Cc

el cangrejo

el canguro

el/la cantante*

la caña de azúcar

la cara

el caracol

los caramelos

la carne

la carretera

el carrito

el carro,
el coche (Méx)

la carta

la cartera

el cartero/la
cartera*

la casa

la caseta del perro

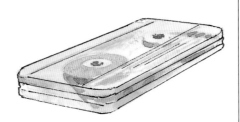

el cassette

la cebolla

la cebra

el cepillo

el cepillo de dientes

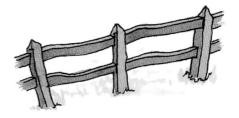

la cerca

Cc

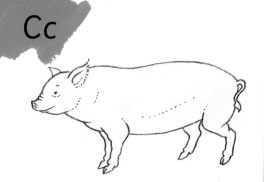

el cerdo

la cesta

el chico

cero

el champú

cerrar

la chaqueta

la chimenea

el cerro

la chica

el chocolate

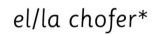

el/la chofer*

el cielo

la ciudad

el científico/la científica*

la clase

el cine

el clavo

la cobija

la cocina

la cocina, la
estufa (Cuba, Méx)

cocinar

el coco

el codo

el cohete

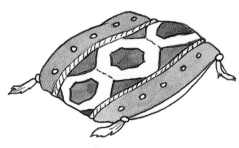

el cojín

la col

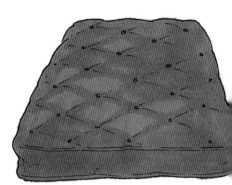

el colchón

el colegio

el colibrí

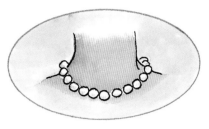

el collar

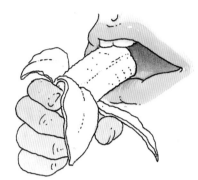

comer

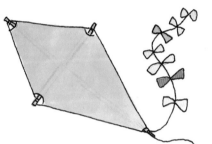

la cometa,
el papalote (Méx)

el cómic

la comida

la computadora

la concha

el conejo

el congelador

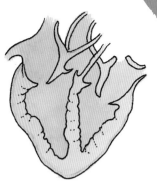

el corazón

la corbata

el cordel

el cordero

el cordón

Cc

la corona

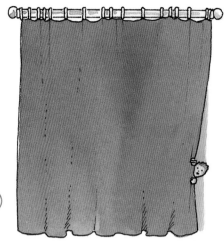

la cortina

el correo

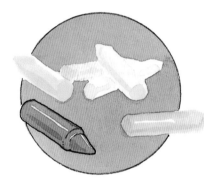

el creyón

la cuadra

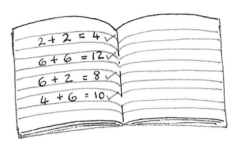

el cuaderno

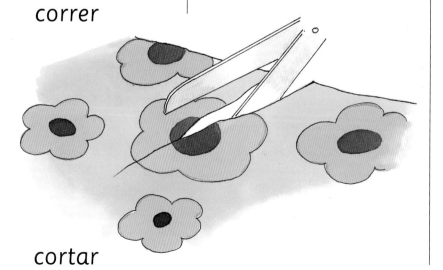

correr

cortar

el cuadro

el críquet

el cuarto, la recámara (Méx)

el cuarto de baño

el cubo

la cuchara

la cucharita

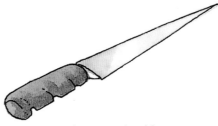

el cuchillo

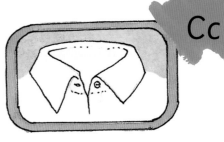

el cuello

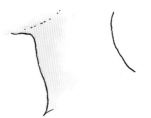

el cuello

la cuerda

el cuerno

el cumpleaños

Dd

decir adiós con la mano

el dedo

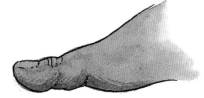

el dedo del pie

el delfín

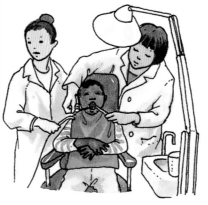

el/la dentista*

el desayuno

el despertador

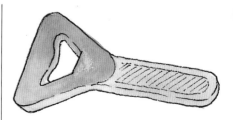

el destapador

dibujar

el dibujo

los dibujos animados

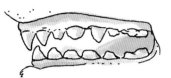

los dientes

el dinero

doblar

el dolor de muelas

el dragón

el dinosaurio

el disquete

dormir

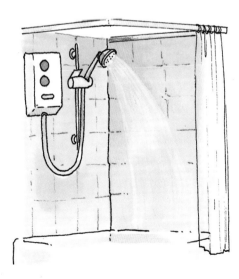

la ducha

Ee

el edificio de
apartamentos

el elefante

el enfermero/la
enfermera*

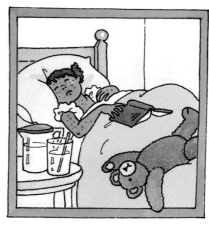

enfermo/enferma*

la ensalada

el equipaje

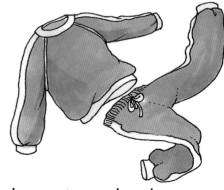

el equipo de deportes
los pants (Méx)

la escalera

la escalera

el escarabajo

escribir

el espacio

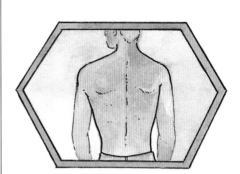

los espaguetis

la espalda

escuchar

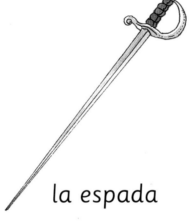

la espada

el espejo

la escuela

la esquina

la estación

la estampilla

el estanque

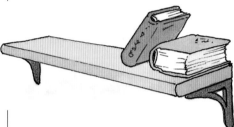

el estante

la estantería

estar de pie

la estrella

la estrella de mar

Ff

la fábrica

la falda

la familia

el fantasma

la flecha

la flor

el florero

la foca

el fósforo,
el cerillo (Méx)

la foto

la frente

los frijoles,
las caraotas (Venz)

Ff

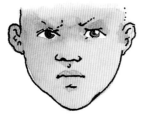

fruncir el ceño

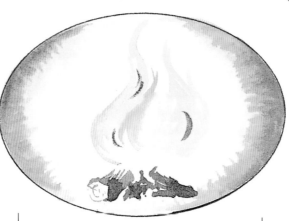

el fuego

la fruta

la fuente

la fuente

la fuente

el fútbol

Gg

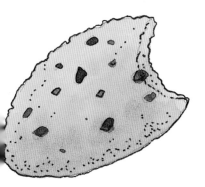

la galleta

la gallina

el gallo

el gancho

el garaje

el gatito

el gato

los gemelos/las gemelas*

el gigante

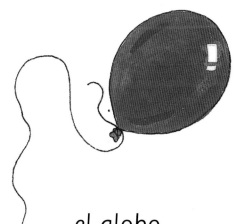

el globo

Gg

el gorila

el granjero/la granjera*

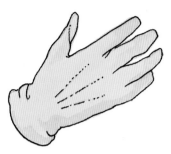

el guante

la guitarra

la grabadora

el guacamayo

el gusano

la granja

Hh

la habitación

el helicóptero

el hacha [F]

las herramientas

el hipopótamo

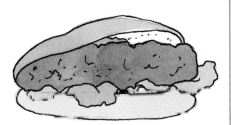

la hamburguesa

el hielo

la hoja

el helado

la hierba

la hoja

Hh

el hombre

el hospital

el hombro

el hueso

el humo

la hormiga

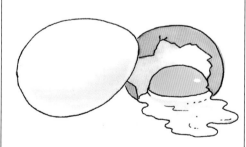

el huevo

el horno

el huracán

Ii

la iglesia

la iguana

el iglú

el imán

el insecto

la isla

Jj

el jabón

la jaula

la joya

el jardín

el jeep

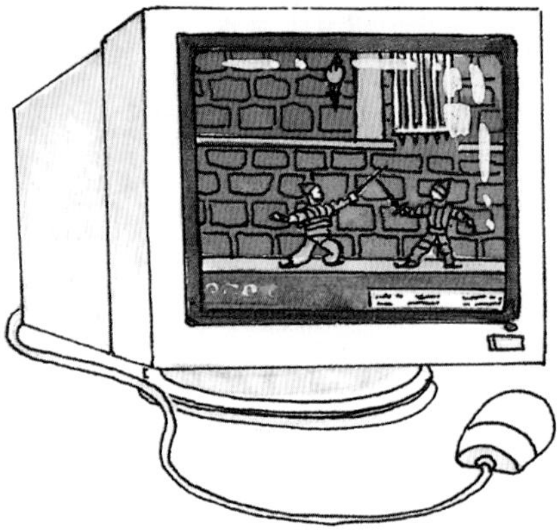

el juego de computadora

la jarra

la jirafa

el jugo

los juguetes

Kk

el kilo

el kilómetro

el kiosco

Ll

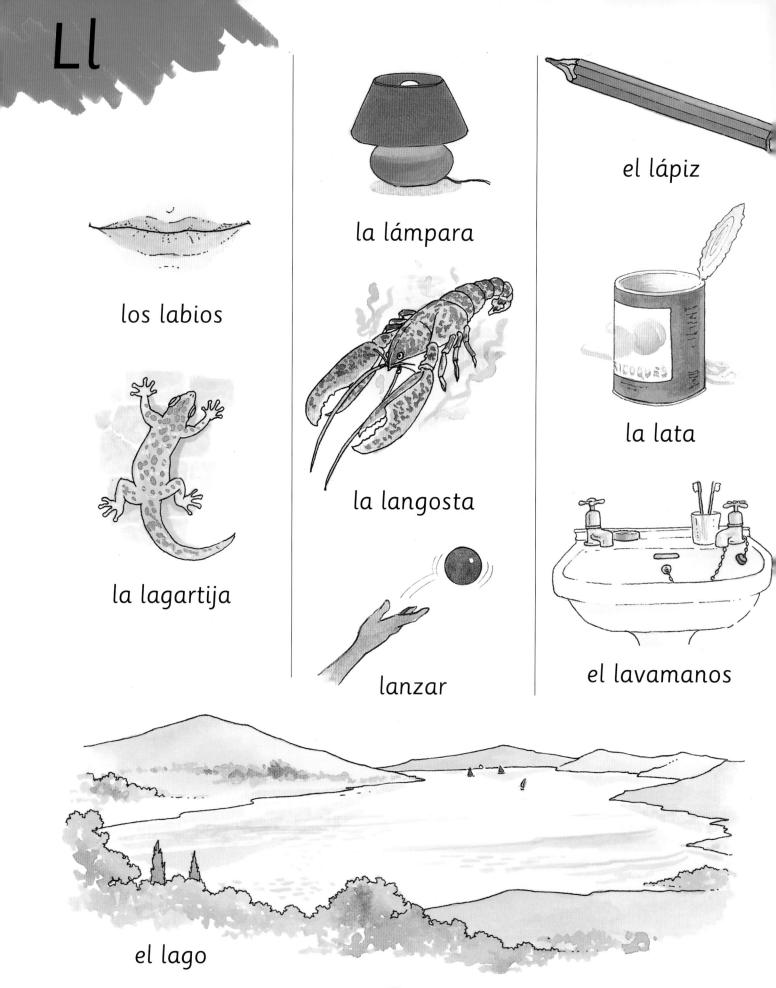

los labios

la lámpara

el lápiz

la lagartija

la langosta

la lata

lanzar

el lavamanos

el lago

50

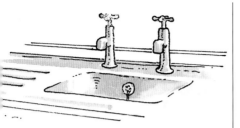

el lavaplatos

la lengua

el león

la leche

los lentes

la lechuga

los lentes de sol

leer

el libro

Ll

ligero/ligera*

el limón

la limonada

la lista

la llave

la llave

la lluvia

la luna

la luz

Mm

el mago/la maga*

el maíz

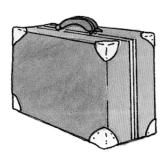

la maleta

manejar

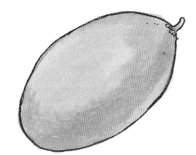

el mango

la mano

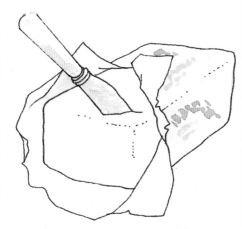

la mantequilla

la manzana

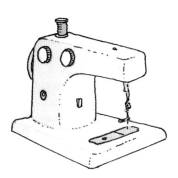

la máquina

el mar

la mariposa

Mm

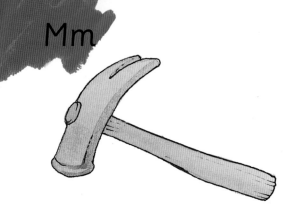

el martillo

la mascarilla

la mata

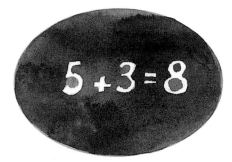

las matemáticas

las medias

la medicina

el médico/la médica*

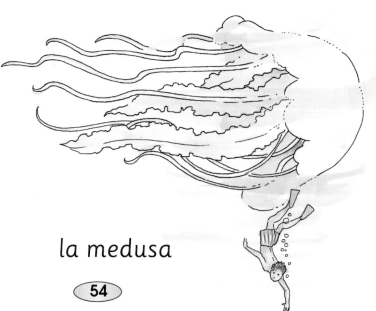

la medusa

el mercado

la mermelada

la mesa

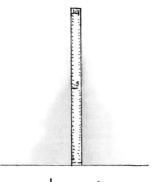

el metro

la mezquita

el monedero

el mono

la montaña

la mosca

la moto

la mujer

la muñeca

el muro

Nn

nadar

la nevera

la niña

naranja

el nido

el niño

la nariz

la nave espacial

la nieve

los niños

el ñame

la nube

la noche

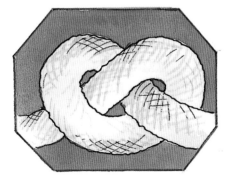

el nudo

57

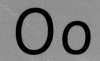

Oo

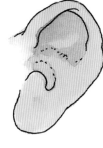

la oreja

el osito de peluche

la oveja

el océano

la oficina

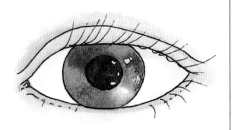

el ojo

Pp

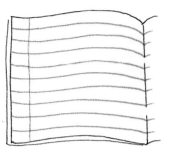

la página

el pájaro

la pala

la palmera

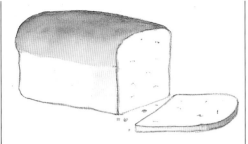

el pan

el panda

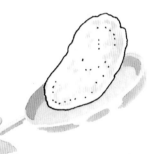

el panqueque,
la crepa (Méx)

los pantalones

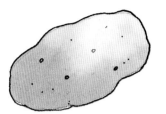

la papa

las papas fritas

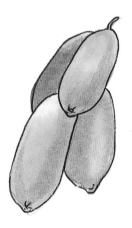

la papaya,
la lechosa (RD, Venz)

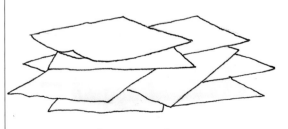

el papel

Pp

la papelera

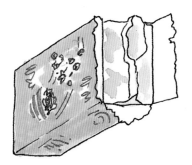

el paquete

el paracaídas

el parque

la parada
de autobuses

el paraguas

la pared

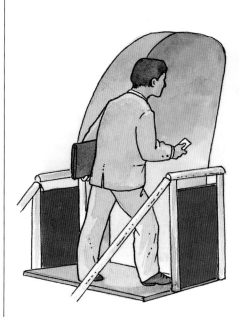

el pasajero/la
pasajera*

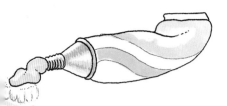

la pasta de dientes

el pavo real

el patito

el pato

la pava, la tetera

el payaso/la payasa*

Pp

el pedal

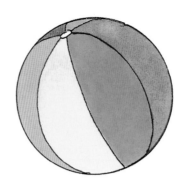

la pelota

el perico

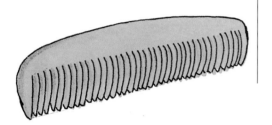

el peine

el periódico

el pelícano

el peluquero/la peluquera*

el perro

el pelo

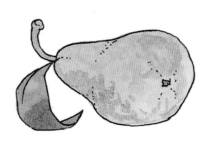

la pera

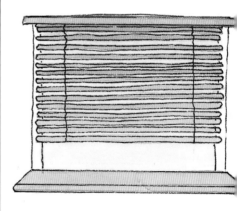

la persiana

una persona

el piano

la pierna

pesado/pesada*

el/la piloto*

el pez

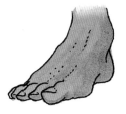

el pie

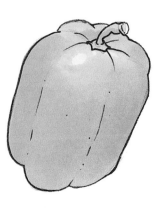

el pimentón

Pp

la pimienta

la piña

la pista de aterrizaje

el pincel

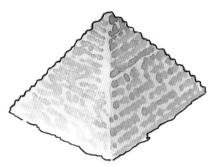

la pirámide

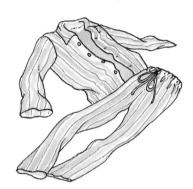

la piyama

el pingüino

la piscina,
la alberca (Méx)

la pizarra

la pintura

el piso

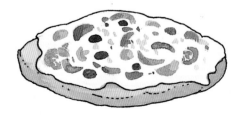

la pizza

64

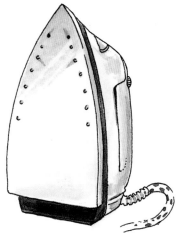

la plancha

el planeta

el plátano (Venz), el
plátano grande (Méx),
el plátano macho
(Méx)

el platillo

la playa

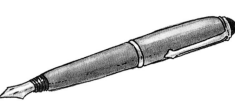

la pluma

la pluma fuente

la población

Pp

el policía/la mujer policía*

el profesor/la profesora*

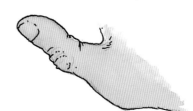

el pulgar

el pulpo

el pollo

el puente

el portón

la puerta

el pupitre

66

Qq

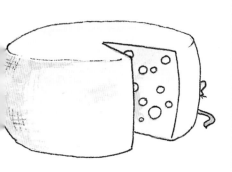

el queso

Rr

el rabo

la rana

el radio

la raqueta

la radiografía

la rama

el ratón

el regalo

el relámpago

el restaurante

la regla

el reloj

la revista

la reina

el remo

el rey

el rincón

las rocas

el rinoceronte

la ropa

la rodilla

el río

la rueda

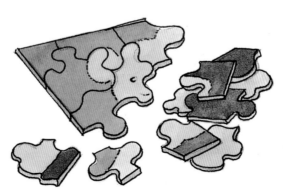

el robot

el rompecabezas

Ss

la salchicha

la sábana

saltar

el salón

el sacapuntas

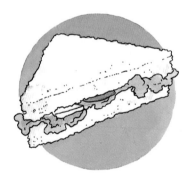

la sandía

la sal

el saltamontes

el sándwich

el secretario/la
secretaria*

la sala

el sol

la selva

el semáforo

la senda

la señal

el short

la silla

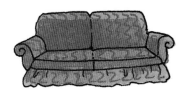

el sofá

la sombra

la sombra

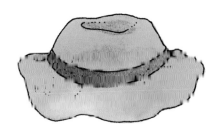

el sombrero

la sombrilla

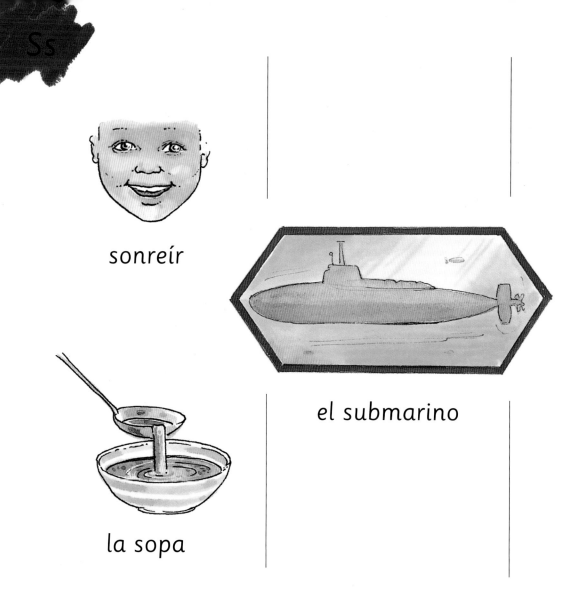

sonreír

el submarino

la sopa

el supermercado

Tt

el tablero de anuncios

el taxi

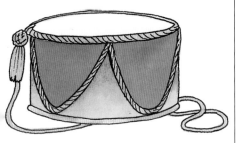

el tambor

la taza

el teléfono

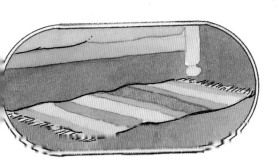

el tapete

el té

el televisor

la tarjeta de cumpleaños

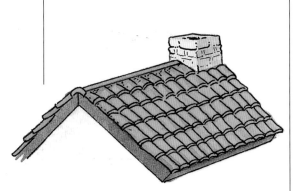

el techo

el templo

Tt

el tenedor

el ternero

la tienda

la tienda de campaña

el tenis

los tenis

el tiburón

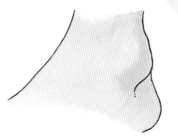

Tt

la tierra

el tobillo

el tomate

el tigre

el toro

las tijeras

la tiza

el títere

la toalla

la torre

Tt

la torta

la tortilla de huevos

la tortuga

las tostadas

el tractor

el tráfico

el traje de baño

el tren

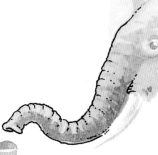

la trompa

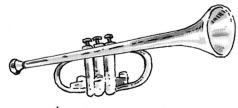

la trompeta

el tronco

el trozo

el/la turista*

76

Uu

la uva

Vv

la vaca

el vaquero

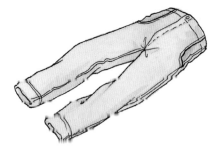

los vaqueros

el vaso

los vegetales

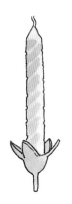

la vela

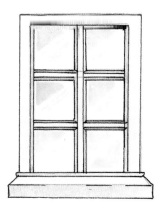

la ventana

Vv

el vestido

el veterinario/la veterinaria*

la víbora

el video

la videocámara

la vieja

el viejo

el viento

el violín

el volcán

Ww

el walkman

el windsurf

Xx

el xilófono

Yy

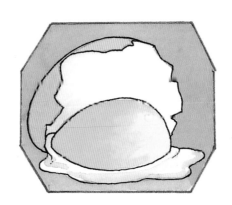

la yema

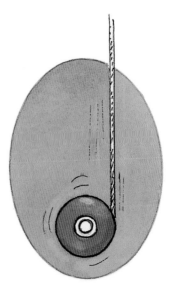

el yo-yo

Zz

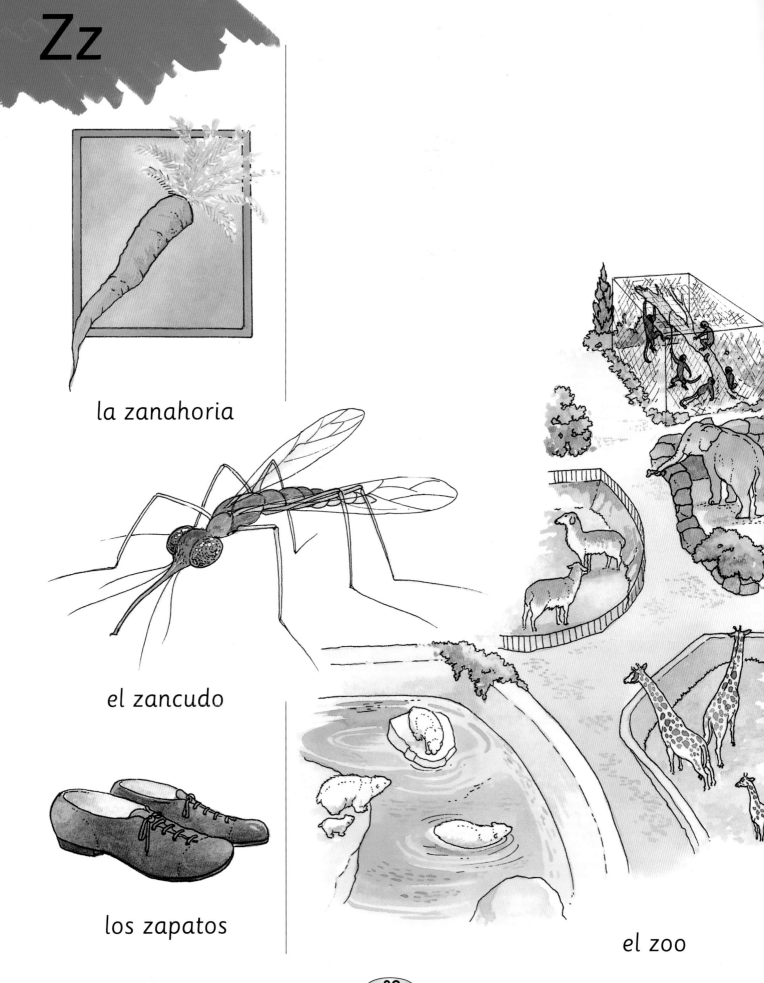

la zanahoria

el zancudo

los zapatos

el zoo

Los números y las fechas

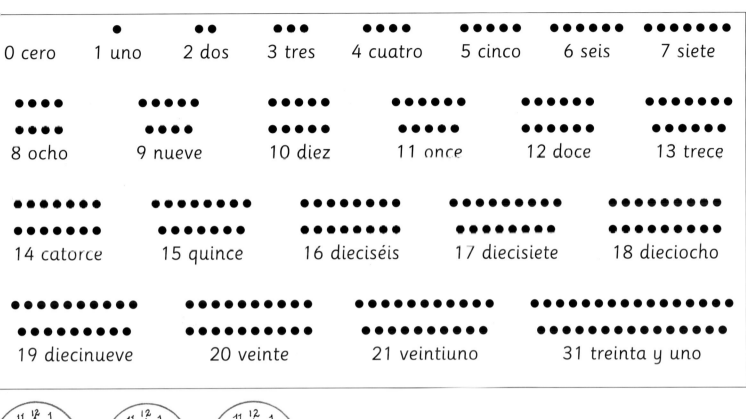

0 cero	1 uno	2 dos	3 tres	4 cuatro	5 cinco	6 seis	7 siete

8 ocho   9 nueve   10 diez   11 once   12 doce   13 trece

14 catorce   15 quince   16 dieciséis   17 diecisiete   18 dieciocho

19 diecinueve   20 veinte   21 veintiuno   31 treinta y uno

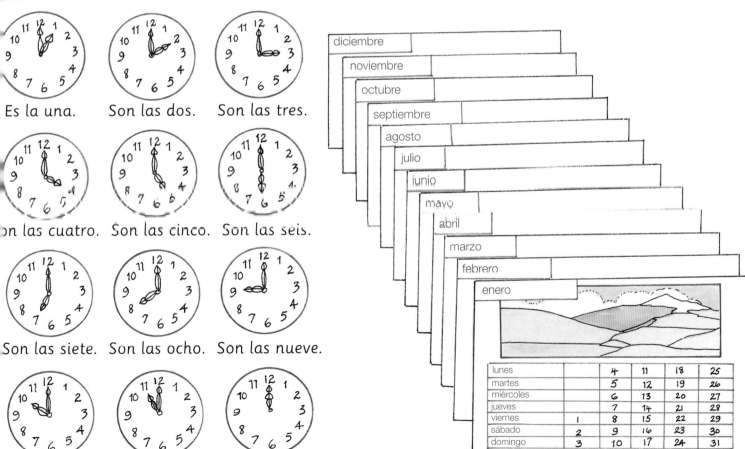

Es la una.   Son las dos.   Son las tres.

Son las cuatro.   Son las cinco.   Son las seis.

Son las siete.   Son las ocho.   Son las nueve.

Son las diez.   Son las once.   Son las doce.

diciembre
noviembre
octubre
septiembre
agosto
julio
junio
mayo
abril
marzo
febrero
enero

lunes		4	11	18	25
martes		5	12	19	26
miércoles		6	13	20	27
jueves		7	14	21	28
viernes	1	8	15	22	29
sábado	2	9	16	23	30
domingo	3	10	17	24	31

Los colores y la ropa

el pincel

negro/
negra*　azul　marrón　verde　gris

la pintura

la caja de
acuarela

naranja　rosado/
rosada*　morado/
morada*　rojo/
roja*　blanco/
blanca*　amarillo/
amarilla*

el nudo

el cuello

el botón

el cordón

el bolsillo

1 la blusa	6 el camisón	10 la falda	16 los vaqueros
2 las botas	7 la chaqueta	11 las medias	17 el vestido
3 la bufanda	8 el collar	12 los pantalones	18 los zapatos
4 la camisa	9 el equipo de	13 la piyama	
5 la camiseta,	deportes, los pants	14 el sombrero	
la franela (Venz)	(Méx)	15 los tenis	

el alumno	7 el lápiz	13 el profesor	19 el tablero
la cartera	8 el libro	14 el pupitre	de anuncios
el creyón	9 la página	15 la regla	20 la tiza
el cuaderno	10 la papelera	16 el sacapuntas	
el dibujo	11 la pizarra	17 el salón	
el estante	12 la pluma fuente	18 la silla	

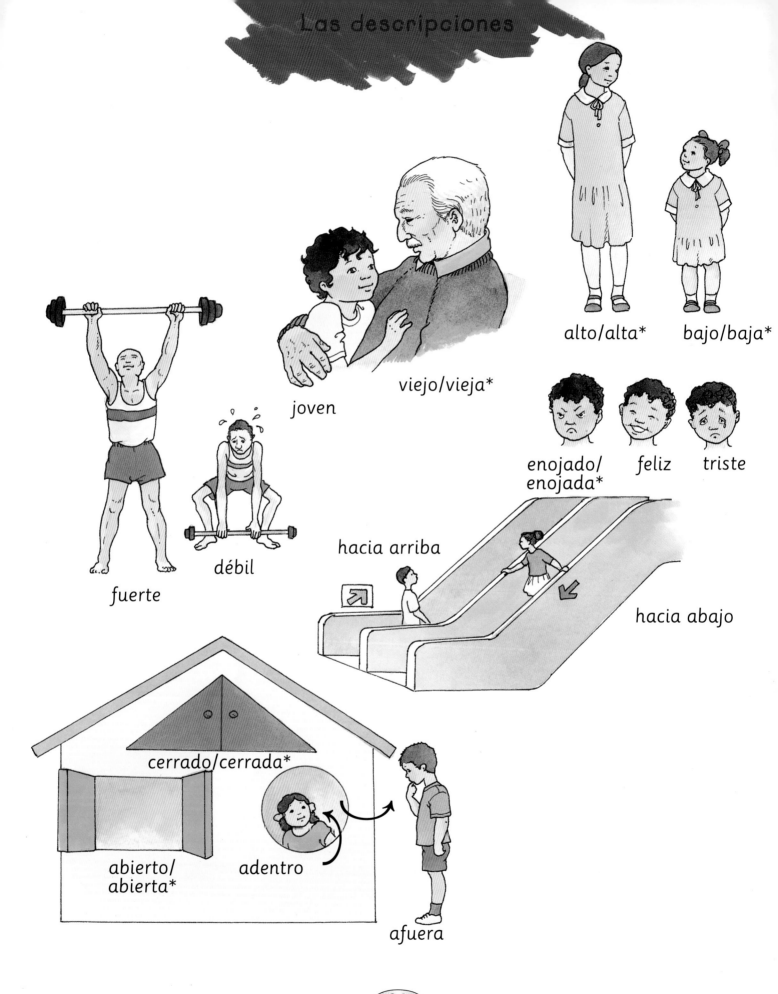

fuerte

débil

joven

viejo/vieja*

alto/alta*   bajo/baja*

enojado/
enojada*   feliz   triste

hacia arriba

hacia abajo

cerrado/cerrada*

abierto/
abierta*   adentro

afuera

la mañana

la tarde

la noche

pesado/
pesada*

ligero/
ligera*

bueno/
buena*

malo/
mala*

encima de

dentro de

sobre

debajo de

gordo/
gorda*

flaco/
flaca*

pequeño/
pequeña*

grande

entre

detrás de

al lado de

delante de

por encima de

caliente

frío/
fría*

limpio/
limpia*

sucio/
sucia*

por debajo de

el círculo

el
cuadrado

el
triángulo

la línea

la estrella

el arco

redondo/
redonda*

alrededor de

Los trabajos

As we saw in the grammar points (page 6), jobs and other words describing people are usually different for a man or a woman. Look at the pictures and see if you can write the name of the job in the table below. Remember, if the picture is of a man you will put *el* and if it is a woman you will put *la*. The first few are done for you. The answers are on page 117.

1 el aeromozo	6 l- c - - - - - - - -	11 -- - - - -	16 -- - - - - - - - - -
2 la artista	7 e- ch - - - -	12 -- - - - - - -	17 -- - - - - - - - -
3 el ast - - - - - - - -	8 l- cient - - - - -	13 -- - - - - - - - - -	18 -- - - - - - - - - - -
4 la ba - - - - - - -	9 -- - - - - - -	14 -- - - - - -	
5 e- bom - - - -	10 -- - - - - - -	15 -- - - - - - - -	

La familia

la gente

las niñas

los chicos

las chicas

los hombres

las mujeres

los niños

los gemelos

los abuelos

el hermano

el esposo

la esposa

el bebé

la hermana

el padre   la madre

los padres

los hijos

el hijo   la hija

En casa

el cuarto,
la recámara
(Méx)

1 la almohada
2 la cama
3 la cobija
4 el colchón
5 el despertador
6 el espejo
7 la luna
8 la persiana
9 la sábana
10 la vela
11 la ventana
12 las zapatillas

la sala

1 la cortina
2 el cuadro
3 la escalera
4 la estantería
5 el llavero
6 el fuego
7 la lámpara
8 el radio
9 la revista
10 el sofá
11 el tapete
12 el teléfono
13 el televisor

El recreo

1 aplaudir
2 bailar
3 el básquetbol
4 el bate
5 el béisbol
6 el críquet
7 la cuerda
8 el fútbol
9 el globo
10 la guitarra
11 el papalote (Méx),
   la cometa
12 la pelota
13 la raqueta
14 el tambor
15 el tenis
16 la trompeta
17 el vaquero
18 el violín
19 el xilófono
20 el yo-yo

ABC

21 la caja
22 el cassette
23 el cómic
24 la computadora
25 los creyones
26 el dinosaurio
27 el disquete
28 el dragón
29 la grabadora
30 el juego de
   computadora
31 los juguetes
32 la muñeca
33 el osito de peluche
34 el papel
35 el payaso
36 el piano
37 el robot
38 el rompecabezas
39 las tijeras
40 el títere

En el campo

1 el árbol
2 el arco iris
3 el barro
4 el bosque
5 el caballo
6 la cabra
7 un campo
8 la cerca
9 el cerdo
10 el cielo
11 el conejo
12 el cordero
13 la flor
14 la gallina
15 la granja
16 el granjero
17 la hierba
18 la hoja
19 el lago
20 la lluvia
21 la montaña

92

22 el nido
23 la nieve
24 la nube
25 la oveja
26 el pájaro
27 el patito
28 el pato
29 el puente
30 la rana
31 el ratón
32 el río
33 el sol
34 el ternero
35 el toro
36 el tractor
37 el tronco
38 la vaca

En la playa

1 la arena
2 el barco de vela
3 beber
4 el bote, la barca
5 el bronceador
6 el buque
7 la cámara
8 la camiseta,
  la franela
  (Venz)
9 el cangrejo
10 la charca
11 comer
12 la concha
13 el cubo
14 los delfines
15 dormir
16 la estrella de
  mar
17 la foto
18 el helado
19 la isla
20 la langosta

21 los lentes de sol
22 el mar
23 la medusa
24 la pala
25 el papalote (Méx),
   la cometa
26 pescar
27 la piscina,
   la alberca (Méx)
28 la playa
29 el pulpo
30 el remo
31 las rocas
32 los sándwiches
33 el short
34 el sol
35 el sombrero
36 la sombrilla
37 la toalla
38 el traje de baño
39 los turistas
40 la videocámara

1 la acera
2 el autobús, el camión (Méx)
 la guagua (Cuba, PtRi)
3 el balcón
4 el banco
5 la bicicleta
6 la bomba de gasolina
7 la calle
8 el camino
9 el camión
10 el carro, el coche (Méx)
11 la carta
12 el cartero
13 la casa
14 la chimenea
15 el cine
16 el correo
17 el edificio de apartamentos
18 la escalera
19 la esquina
20 la estación

21 la fábrica
22 la fuente
23 la furgoneta
24 la iglesia
25 el kiosco
26 el letrero
27 el mercado
28 la mezquita
29 la moto
30 la oficina
31 la parada
32 el parque
33 el periódico
34 el restaurante
35 el semáforo
36 el taxi
37 el techo
38 la tienda
39 el tráfico
40 el tren

En el supermercado

1 los aguacates
2 los albaricoques
3 las bananas,
   los cambures (Venz),
   los guineos (Cuba, PtRi),
   los plátanos (Méx)
4 las botellas
5 los botes
6 la cajera
7 los caramelos
8 la carne
9 el carrito
10 las cebollas
11 las cestas
12 el chocolate
13 los cocos
14 la comida
15 el congelador
16 el dinero
17 la fruta
18 los huevos
19 las latas
20 la leche

VEGETALES

SUPE

FRUTA

21 las lechugas
22 los limones
23 los mangos
24 la mantequilla
25 las manzanas
26 el monedero
27 las naranjas
28 el pan
29 las papas
30 las papayas,
   las lechosas (RD,
   Venz)
31 los paquetes
32 las peras
33 las piñas
34 los plátanos
   (Venz),
   los plátanos
   grandes (Méx),
   los plátanos
   machos (Méx)
35 el queso
36 las sandías
37 los tomates
38 las uvas
39 los vegetales
40 las zanahorias

En el hospital

1 la barba	11 el cuello	21 el hueso	31 el parche
2 la barbilla	12 el cuerpo	22 los labios	32 el peine
3 la boca	13 el dedo	23 la lengua	33 el pelo
4 el brazo	14 el dedo del pie	24 la mano	34 el pie
5 la cabeza	15 la dentista	25 la mascarilla	35 la pierna
6 la cara	16 el diente	26 la medicina	36 el pulgar
7 el cepillo	17 el dolor de muelas	27 el médico	37 la radiografía
8 el cerebro	18 la enfermera	28 la nariz	38 el reloj
9 el codo	19 la frente	29 el ojo	39 la rodilla
10 el corazón	20 el hombro	30 la oreja	40 el tobillo

101

En el aeropuerto

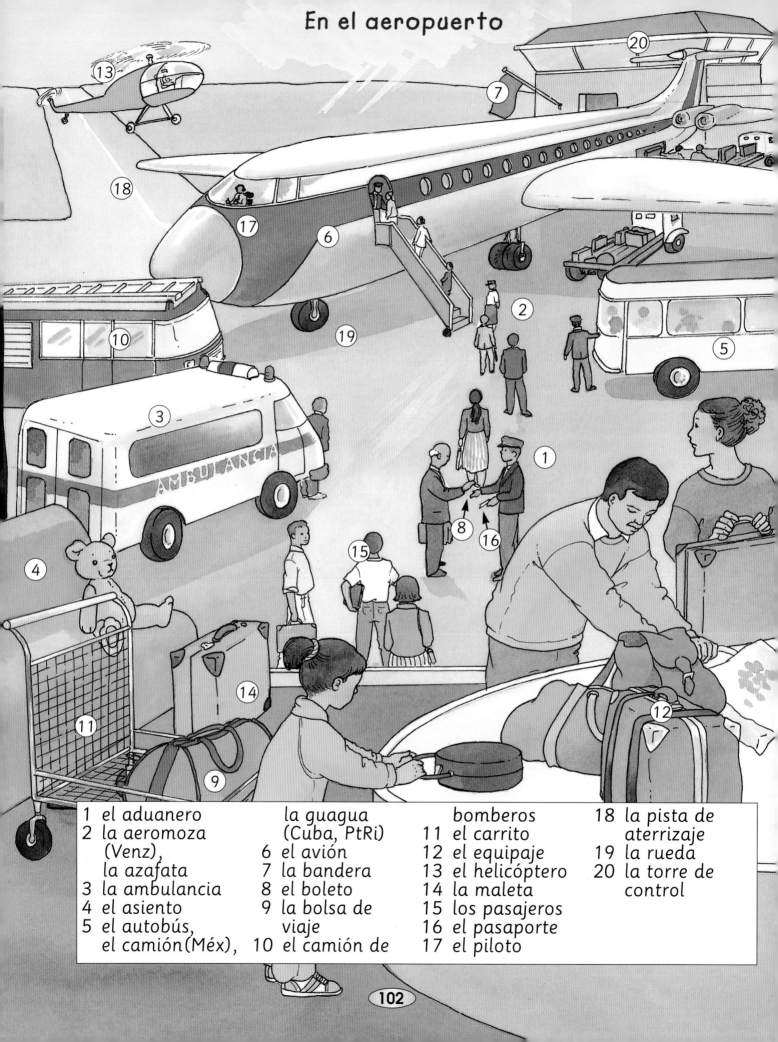

1	el aduanero		la guagua		bomberos	18	la pista de
2	la aeromoza		(Cuba, PtRi)	11	el carrito		aterrizaje
	(Venz),	6	el avión	12	el equipaje	19	la rueda
	la azafata	7	la bandera	13	el helicóptero	20	la torre de
3	la ambulancia	8	el boleto	14	la maleta		control
4	el asiento	9	la bolsa de	15	los pasajeros		
5	el autobús,		viaje	16	el pasaporte		
	el camión(Méx),	10	el camión de	17	el piloto		

¡Feliz cumpleaños!

1 los cubitos de hielo	7 la limonada	11 la pimienta	18 la tarjeta de cumpleaños
2 la ensalada	8 los maníes, los cacahuetes (Méx)	12 la pizza	19 la torta
3 los espaguetis		13 el pollo	20 el trozo de torta
4 la galleta	9 las palomitas de maíz	14 el regalo	
5 la hamburguesa		15 la sal	
6 el helado	10 las papas fritas	16 la salchicha	
		17 el sándwich	

Los animales

1 el águila [F]
2 la araña
3 el avestruz
4 la ballena
5 el caimán
6 el camello
7 el canguro
8 el caracol
9 la cebra
10 el elefante
11 el escarabajo
12 la foca
13 el gorila
14 el gusano
15 el hipopótamo
16 la jirafa
17 la lagartija
18 el león
19 el lobo
20 la mariposa
21 el mono
22 la mosca
23 el oso
24 el panda
25 el pavo real
26 el perico
27 el pez
28 el pingüino
29 el rinoceronte
30 el saltamontes
31 el tiburón
32 el tigre
33 la tortuga
34 la víbora
35 el zancudo

104

Wordlists

These wordlists (Spanish–English and English–Spanish) contain all the words in both the alphabetical section as well as the theme pages.

* = masculine and feminine have different forms

[F] = a feminine word that is used with _el_.

Spanish	English

Aa

la abeja	bee
abierto/abierta*	open
el abrelatas	can opener
el abrigo	coat
abril	April
abrir	to open
la abuela	grandmother
el abuelo	grandfather
los abuelos	grandparents
la acera	pavement
adentro	inside
el aduanero/la aduanera*	customs officer
el aeromozo/ la aeromoza*	flight attendant
el aeropuerto	airport
afuera	outside
agarrar	to catch
la agenda	diary
agosto	August
el agua [F]	water
el aguacate	avocado
el águila [F]	eagle
la aguja	needle
al lado de	next to
el albaricoque	apricot
la alberca (Méx)	swimming pool
el alfabeto	alphabet
el alfiler	pin
la almohada	pillow

el almuerzo	lunch
alrededor de	around
alto/alta*	tall; high
el alumno/ la alumna*	pupil
amarillo/amarilla*	yellow
la ambulancia	ambulance
el anillo	ring
el animal	animal
aplaudir	clap
la araña	spider
el árbol	tree
el arco	arc
el arco iris	rainbow
la arena	sand
el armario	cupboard
el arroz	rice
el/la artista*	artist
el asiento	seat
la aspiradora	vacuum cleaner
el/la astronauta*	astronaut
el/la atleta*	athlete
el autobús	bus
el avestruz	ostrich
el avión	plane
la azafata	flight attendant
el azúcar	sugar
azul	blue

Bb

bailar	to dance
el bailarín/ la bailarina*	dancer
el balcón	balcony
la ballena	whale
el baloncesto (Cuba)	basketball
la banana	banana
el banco	bank; bench
la bandera	flag
la bañera	bath
la barba	beard
la barbilla	chin
la barca	boat
el barco de vela	sailboat

el barro	mud
el básquetbol	basketball
el bastón	walking stick
el bate	bat
el bebé	baby
beber	to drink
el béisbol	baseball
la biblioteca	library
la bicicleta	bicycle
el bigote	moustache
el bikini	bikini
blanco/blanca*	white
la blusa	blouse
la boca	mouth
el bol	bowl
el boleto	ticket
el bolígrafo	ballpoint pen
la bolsa de viaje	bag
el bolsillo	pocket
la bomba de gasolina	filling station
el/la bombero*	fire-fighter
las botas	boots
el bote	boat; jar
la botella	bottle
el botón	button
el brazo	arm
el bronceador	suntan oil
bueno/buena*	good
la bufanda	scarf
el buque	ship

Cc

el caballo	horse
la cabeza	head
la cabra	goat
los cacahuetes (Méx)	peanuts
la cacerola	pan
el cachorro	puppy
el café	coffee
el caimán	alligator
la caja	box
la caja de acuarelas	paintbox

el cajero/la cajera*	cashier
el calendario	calendar
caliente	hot
la calle	street
la cama	bed
la cámara	camera
el cambur (Venz)	banana
el camello	camel
caminar	to walk
el camino	path, track
el camión	trunk
el camión (Méx)	bus
el camión de bomberos	fire engine
la camioneta	van
la camisa	shirt
la camiseta	T shirt
el camisón	nightdress
la campana	bell
el campo	countryside
un campo	field
el cangrejo	crab
el canguro	kangaroo
el/la cantante*	singer
la caña de azúcar	sugar cane
la cara	face
el caracol	snail
los caramelos	candy
las caraotas (Venz)	refried beans
la carne	meat
la carretera	main road
el carrito	trolley
el carro	car
la carta	letter
la cartera	schoolbag
el cartero/la cartera*	postman/woman
la casa	house
la caseta del perro	kennel
el cassette	cassette tape
la cebolla	onion
la cebra	zebra
el cepillo	hairbrush
el cepillo de dientes	toothbrush
la cerca	fence
el cerdo	pig
el cerebro	brain
el cerillo (Méx)	match
cero	zero
cerrado/cerrada*	closed
cerrar	to close
el cerro	hill
la cesta	basket
el champú	shampoo
la chaqueta	jacket
la charca	pool
la chica	girl, young woman
el chico	boy, young man
la chimenea	chimney
el chocolate	chocolate
el/la chofer*	driver
el cielo	sky
el científico/la científica*	scientist
el cine	cinema
el círculo	circle
la ciudad	city
la clase	class, lesson
el clavo	nail
la cobija	blanket
el coche (Méx)	car
la cocina	cooker; kitchen
cocinar	to cook
el coco	coconut
el codo	elbow
el cohete	rocket
el cojín	cushion
la col	cabbage
el colchón	mattress
el colegio	secondary school
el colibrí	humming bird
el collar	necklace
el color	colour
comer	to eat
la cometa	kite
el cómic	comic
la comida	food; evening meal
la computadora	computer
la concha	shell
el conejo	rabbit
el congelador	freezer
el corazón	heart
la corbata	tie
el cordel	string
el cordero	lamb
el cordón	lace
la corona	crown
el correo	post office
correr	to run
cortar	to cut
la cortina	curtain
la crepa (Méx)	pancake
el creyón	crayon
el críquet	cricket
el cuaderno	notebook
la cuadra	stables
el cuadrado	square
el cuadro	picture
el cuarto	bedroom
el cuarto de baño	bathroom
el cubito de hielo	ice cube
el cubo	bucket
la cuchara	spoon
la cucharita	tea spoon
el cuchillo	knife
el cuello	collar; neck
la cuerda	rope
el cuerno	horn
el cuerpo	body
el cumpleaños	birthday

Dd

debajo de	underneath
débil	weak
decir adiós con la mano	to wave goodbye
el dedo	finger
el dedo del pie	toe
delante de	in front of
el delfín	dolphin
el/la dentista*	dentist
el desayuno	breakfast
el despertador	alarm clock
el destapador	bottle opener
detrás de	behind
dibujar	to draw
el dibujo	drawing
los dibujos animados	cartoon
diciembre	December
los dientes	teeth
el dinero	money
el dinosaurio	dinosaur
el disquete	floppy disk
doblar	to fold
el dolor de muelas	toothache
domingo	Sunday
dormir	sleep
el dragón	dragon
la ducha	shower

Ee

el edificio de apartamentos	apartment block
el elefante	elephant

en	in; on	la frente	forehead	la hierba	grass
encima de	on top of; over	los frijoles	refried beans	la hija	daughter
enero	January	frío/fría*	cold	el hijo	son
el enfermero/		fruncir el ceño	to frown	el hipopótamo	hippopotamus
la enfermera*	nurse	la fruta	fruit	la hoja	leaf; sheet of
enfermo/enferma*	ill	el fuego	fire		paper
enojado/enojada*	angry	la fuente	dish; fountain	el hombre	man
la ensalada	salad	fuerte	strong	el hombro	shoulder
entre	between	el fútbol	football	la hormiga	ant
el equipaje	baggage			el horno	oven
el equipo de		**Gg**		el hospital	hospital
deportes	tracksuit	la galleta	biscuit	el hueso	bone
la escalera	ladder; stairs	la gallina	hen	el huevo	egg
el escarabajo	beetle	el gallo	cockerel	el humo	smoke
escribir	to write	el gancho	hook	el huracán	hurricane
escuchar	to listen	el garaje	garage		
la escuela	school	el gatito	kitten	**Ii**	
el espacio	space	el gato	cat	la iglesia	church
la espada	sword	los gemelos/		el iglú	igloo
los espaguetis	spaghetti	las gemelas*	twins	la iguana	iguana
la espalda	back	la gente	people	el imán	magnet
el espejo	mirror	el gigante	giant	el insecto	insect
la esposa	wife	el globo	balloon	la isla	island
el esposo	husband	gordo/gorda*	fat		
la esquina	corner (of a	el gorila	gorilla	**Jj**	
	street)	la grabadora	cassette player	el jabón	soap
la estación	station	grande	big	el jardín	garden
la estampilla	stamp	la granja	farm	la jarra	jug
el estanque	pond	el granjero/		la jaula	cage
el estante	shelf	la granjera*	farmer	el jeep	jeep
la estantería	bookcase	gris	grey	la jirafa	giraffe
estar de pie	to stand	el guacamayo	macaw	joven	young
la estrella	star	la guagua		la joya	jewel
la estrella de mar	starfish	(Cuba, PtRi)	bus	el juego de	computer
la estufa		el guante	glove	computadora	game
(Cuba, Méx)	cooker	el guineo (PtRi)	banana	jueves	Thursday
		la guitarra	guitar	el jugo	juice
Ff		el gusano	worm	los juguetes	toys
la fábrica	factory			julio	July
la falda	skirt	**Hh**		junio	June
la familia	family	la habitación	room		
el fantasma	ghost	el hacha [F]	axe	**Kk**	
febrero	February	hacia abajo	down	el kilo	kilo
feliz	happy	hacia arriba	up	el kilómetro	kilometre
¡feliz cumpleaños!	happy birthday!	la hamburguesa	hamburger	el kiosco	newspaper
flaco/flaca*	thin	el helado	ice-cream		stand
la flecha	arrow	el helicóptero	helicopter		
la flor	flower	la hermana	sister	**Ll**	
el florero	vase	el hermano	brother	los labios	lips
la foca	seal	los hermanos	brothers and	la lagartija	lizard
el fósforo	match		sisters	el lago	lake
la foto	photo	las herramientas	tools	la lámpara	lamp
la franela (Venz)	T-shirt	el hielo	ice	la langosta	lobster

lanzar	to throw	las matemáticas	mathematics	el oso	bear
el lápiz	pencil	mayo	May	la oveja	sheep
la lata	can	las medias	socks		
el lavamanos	wash basin	la medicina	medicine		

lanzar — to throw
el lápiz — pencil
la lata — can
el lavamanos — wash basin
el lavaplatos — sink
la leche — milk
la lechosa (RD, Venz) — pawpaw
la lechuga — lettuce
leer — to read
la lengua — tongue
los lentes — glasses
los lentes de sol — sunglasses
el león — lion
el letrero — sign, notice
el libro — book
ligero/ligera* — light (not heavy)
el limón — lime
la limonada — lemonade
limpio/limpia* — clean
la línea — line
la lista — list
la llave — key; tap
la lluvia — rain
el lobo — wolf
la luna — moon
lunes — Monday
la luz — light (daylight, electric light)

Mm

la madre — mother
el mago/la maga* — magician
el maíz — corn
la maleta — suitcase
malo/mala* — bad
manejar — to drive
el maní — money
los maníes — peanuts
la mano — hand
la mantequilla — butter
la manzana — apple
la mañana — morning
la máquina — machine
el mar — sea
la mariposa — butterfly
marrón — brown
martes — Tuesday
el martillo — hammer
marzo — March
la mascarilla — mask
la mata — plant

las matemáticas — mathematics
mayo — May
las medias — socks
la medicina — medicine
el médico/la médica* — doctor
la medusa — jellyfish
el mercado — market
la mermelada — jam
la mesa — table
el metro — metre
la mezquita — mosque
miércoles — Wednesday
el monedero — purse
el mono — monkey
la montaña — mountain
morado/morada* — purple
la mosca — fly
la moto — motorcycle
la mujer — woman
la mujer policía — policewoman
la muñeca — doll
el muro — wall (outside of house)

Nn

nadar — to swim
naranja — orange (colour)
la naranja — orange (fruit)
la nariz — nose
la nave espacial — spaceship
negro/negra* — black
la nevera — refrigerator
el nido — nest
la nieve — snow
la niña — girl
el niño — boy
los niños — children
la noche — night
noviembre — November
la nube — cloud
el nudo — knot

Ññ

el ñame — yam

Oo

el océano — ocean
octubre — October
la oficina — office
el ojo — eye
la oreja — ear
el osito de peluche — teddy bear

el oso — bear
la oveja — sheep

Pp

el padre — father
los padres — parents
la página — page
el pájaro — bird
la pala — spade
la palmera — palm tree
las palomitas de maíz — popcorn
el pan — bread
el panda — panda
el panqueque — pancake
los pantalones — trousers
los pants (Mex) — tracksuit
el paño — tea towel
la papa — potato
el papalote (Méx) — kite
las papas fritas — French fries
la papaya — pawpaw
el papel — paper
la papelera — wastepaper basket
el paquete — packet
el paracaídas — parachute
la parada de autobuses — bus stop
el paraguas — umbrella
el parche — eye patch
la pared — wall (inside house)
el parque — park
el pasajero/la pasajera* — passenger
el pasaporte — passport
la pasta de dientes — toothpaste
el patito — duckling
el pato — duck
la pava — kettle
el pavo real — peacock
el payaso/la payasa* — clown
el pedal — pedal
el peine — comb
el pelícano — pelican
el pelo — hair
la pelota — ball
el peluquero/la peluquera* — hairdresser
pequeño/pequeña* — small
la pera — pear

el perico	parrot			el semáforo	traffic lights
el periódico	newspaper			la senda	path
el perro	dog			la señal	sign, signal
la persiana	blind			septiembre	September
una persona	person			el short	shorts
pesado/pesada*	heavy			la silla	chair
pescar	to fish			sobre	on
el pez	fish (live)			el sofá	sofa
el piano	piano			el sol	sun
el pie	foot			la sombra	shade; shadow
la pierna	leg			el sombrero	hat
el/la piloto*	pilot			la sombrilla	sunshade
el pimentón	capsicum			sonreír	to smile
la pimienta	pepper (ground)			la sopa	soup
el pincel	paintbrush			el submarino	submarine
el pingüino	penguin			sucio/sucia*	dirty
la pintura	paint			el supermercado	supermarket
la piña	pineapple				

el queso	cheese

el rabo	tail
el radio	radio
la radiografía	X-ray
la rama	branch
la rana	frog
la raqueta	racket
el ratón	mouse
la recámara (Méx)	bedroom
el recreo	play time
redondo/redonda*	round
el regalo	present
la regla	ruler
la reina	queen
el relámpago	lightning
el reloj	watch
el remo	oar
el restaurante	restaurant
la revista	magazine
el rey	king
el rincón	corner (of a room)
el rinoceronte	rhinoceros
el río	river
el robot	robot
las rocas	rocks
la rodilla	knee
rojo/roja*	red
el rompecabezas	puzzle
la ropa	clothes
rosado/rosada*	pink
la rueda	wheel

sábado	Saturday
la sábana	sheet
el sacapuntas	pencil sharpener
la sal	salt
la sala	living room
la salchicha	sausage
el salón	classroom
el saltamontes	grasshopper
saltar	to jump
la sandía	water melon
el sándwich	sandwich
la sartén	frying pan
el secretario/ la secretaria*	secretary
la selva	jungle

la pirámide	pyramid
la piscina	swimming pool
el piso	floor
la pista de aterrizaje	runway
la piyama	pyjamas
la pizarra	blackboard
la pizza	pizza
la plancha	iron
el planeta	planet
el plátano (Méx)	banana
el plátano (Venz)	plantain
el plátano grande (Méx)	plantain
el plátano macho (Méx)	plantain
el platillo	saucer
el plato	plate
la playa	beach
la pluma	feather
la pluma fuente	fountain pen
la población	town
el policía	policeman
el pollo	chicken
por debajo de	(go) under
por encima de	(go) over
el portón	gate
el profesor/ la profesora*	teacher
el puente	bridge
la puerta	door
el pulgar	thumb
el pulpo	octopus
el pupitre	desk

el tablero de anuncios	noticeboard
el tambor	drum
el tapete	rug
la tarde	afternoon; evening
la tarjeta de cumpleaños	birthday card
el taxi	taxi
la taza	cup
el té	tea
el techo	roof
el teléfono	telephone
el televisor	television
el templo	temple
el tenedor	fork
el tenis	tennis
los tenis	trainers
el ternero	calf
la tetera	kettle
el tiburón	shark
la tienda	shop
la tienda de campaña	tent
la tierra	earth
el tigre	tiger
las tijeras	scissors
el títere	puppet
la tiza	chalk
la toalla	towel
el tobillo	ankle
el tomate	tomato
el toro	bull
la torre	tower

la torre de control	control tower
la torta	cake
la tortilla de huevos	omelette
la tortuga	tortoise
las tostadas	toast
el tractor	tractor
el tráfico	traffic
el traje de baño	swimming trunks; swimsuit
el tren	train
el triángulo	triangle
triste	sad
la trompa	elephant's trunk
la trompeta	trumpet
el tronco	tree trunk
el trozo	slice
el/la turista*	tourist

Uu

la uva	grape

Vv

la vaca	cow
el vaquero	cowboy
los vaqueros	jeans
el vaso	glass
los vegetales	vegetables
la vela	candle
la ventana	window
verde	green
el vestido	dress
el veterinario/ la veterinaria*	vet
la víbora	snake
el video	video (recorder and tape)
la videocámara	camcorder
la vieja	old woman
el viejo	old man
viejo/vieja*	old
el viento	wind
viernes	Friday
el violín	violin
el volcán	volcano

Ww

el walkman	walkman
el windsurf	windsurfing

Xx

el xilófono	xylophone

Yy

la yema	yolk (of egg)
el yo-yo	yo-yo

Zz

la zanahoria	carrot
el zancudo	mosquito
los zapatos	shoes
el zoo	zoo

English	Spanish

A

afternoon	la tarde
airport	el aeropuerto
alarm clock	el despertador
alligator	el caimán
alphabet	el alfabeto
ambulance	la ambulancia
angry	enojado/ enojada*
animal	el animal
ankle	el tobillo
ant	la hormiga
apartment block	el edificio de apartamentos
apple	la manzana
apricot	el albaricoque
April	abril
arc	el arco
arm	el brazo
around	alrededor de
arrow	la flecha
artist	el/la artista*
astronaut	el/la astronauta*
athlete	el/la atleta
August	agosto
avocado	el aguacate
axe	el hacha [F]

Bb

baby	el bebé
back	la espalda
bad	malo/mala*
bag	la bolsa de viaje
baggage	el equipaje
balcony	el balcón
ball	la pelota
balloon	el globo
ballpoint pen	el bolígrafo
banana	la banana; el cambur (Venz); el guineo (PtRi); el plátano (Méx)
bank	el banco
baseball	el béisbol
basket	la cesta
basketball	el básquetbol; el baloncesto (Cuba)
bat	el bate
bath	la bañera
bathroom	el cuarto de baño
beach	la playa
bear	el oso
beard	la barba
bed	la cama
bedroom	el cuarto; la recámara (Méx)
bee	la abeja
beetle	el escarabajo
behind	detrás de
bell	la campana
bench	el banco
between	entre
bicycle	la bicicleta
big	grande
bikini	el bikini
bird	el pájaro
birthday	el cumpleaños
birthday card	la tarjeta de cumpleaños
biscuit	la galleta
black	negro/negra*
blackboard	la pizarra
blanket	la cobija
blind	la persiana
blouse	la blusa
blue	azul
boat	el bote; la barca
body	el cuerpo
bone	el hueso
book	el libro
bookcase	la estantería
boots	las botas

bottle	la botella	chalk	la tiza	curtain	la cortina
bottle opener	el destapador	cheese	el queso	cushion	el cojín
bowl	el bol	chicken	el pollo	customs officer	el aduanero/la
box	la caja	children	los niños		aduanera*
boy	el niño	chimney	la chimenea	cut, to	cortar
boy (young man)	el chico	chin	la barbilla		
brain	el cerebro	chocolate	el chocolate	**Dd**	
branch	la rama	church	la iglesia	dance, to	bailar
bread	el pan	cicada	la chicharra	dancer	el bailarín/la
breakfast	el desayuno	cinema	el cine		bailarina*
bridge	el puente	circle	el círculo	daughter	la hija
brother	el hermano	city	la ciudad	December	diciembre
brothers and		clap	aplaudir	dentist	el/la dentista*
sisters	los hermanos	class	la clase	desk	el pupitre
brown	marrón	classroom	el salón	diary	la agenda
bucket	el cubo	clean	limpio/limpia*	dinosaur	el dinosaurio
bull	el toro	close, to	cerrar	dirty	sucio/sucia*
bus	el autobús; el	closed	cerrado/	dish	la fuente
	camión (Méx);		cerrada*	doctor	el médico/la
	la guagua	clothes	la ropa		médica*
	(Cuba, PtRi)	cloud	la nube	dog	el perro
bus stop	la parada	clown	el payaso/	doll	la muñeca
	de autobuses		la payasa*	dolphin	el delfín
butter	la mantequilla	coat	el abrigo	door	la puerta
butterfly	la mariposa	cockerel	el gallo	down	hacia abajo
button	el botón	coconut	el coco	dragon	el dragón
		coffee	el café	draw, to	dibujar
Cc		cold	frío/fría*	drawing	el dibujo
cabbage	la col	collar	el cuello	dress	el vestido
cage	la jaula	colour	el color	drink, to	beber
cake	la torta	comb	el peine	drive, to	manejar
calendar	el calendario	comic	el cómic	driver	el/la chofer*
calf	el ternero	computer	la computadora	drum	el tambor
camcorder	la videocámara	computer game	el juego de	duck	el pato
camel	el camello		computadora	duckling	el patito
camera	la cámara	control tower	la torre de		
can	la lata		control	**Ee**	
can opener	el abrelatas	cook, to	cocinar	eagle	el águila [F]
candle	la vela	cooker	la cocina; la	ear	la oreja
candy	los caramelos		estufa (Cuba,	earth	la tierra
capsicum	el pimentón		Méx)	eat, to	comer
car	el carro; el	corn	el maíz	egg	el huevo
	coche (Méx)	corner (of a room)	el rincón	elbow	el codo
carrot	la zanahoria	corner (of a street)	la esquina	elephant	el elefante
cartoon	los dibujos	countryside	el campo	elephant's trunk	la trompa
	animados	cow	la vaca	evening	la tarde
cashier	el cajero/la	cowboy	el vaquero	evening meal	la comida
	cajera*	crab	el cangrejo	eye	el ojo
cassette player	la grabadora	crayon	el creyón	eye patch	el parche
cassette tape	el cassette	cricket	el críquet		
cat	el gato	crown	la corona	**Ff**	
catch, to	agarrar	cup	la taza	face	la cara
chair	la silla	cupboard	el armario	factory	la fábrica

family	la familia
farm	la granja
farmer	el granjero/la granjera*
fat	gordo/gorda*
father	el padre
feather	la pluma
February	febrero
fence	la cerca
field	un campo
filling station	la bomba de gasolina
finger	el dedo
fire	el fuego
fire engine	el camión de bomberos
fire-fighter	el/la bombero*
fish (live)	el pez
fish, to	pescar
flag	la bandera
flight attendant	el aeromozo/la aeromoza*/la azafata
floor	el piso
floppy disk	el disquete
flower	la flor
fly	la mosca
fold, to	doblar
food	la comida
foot	el pie
football	el fútbol
forehead	la frente
fork	el tenedor
fountain	la fuente
fountain pen	la pluma fuente
freezer	el congelador
French fries	las papas fritas
Friday	viernes
frog	la rana
frown, to	fruncir el ceño
fruit	la fruta
frying pan	la sartén

Gg

garage	el garaje
garden	el jardín
gate	el portón
ghost	el fantasma
giant	el gigante
giraffe	la jirafa
girl	la niña
girl, young woman	la chica

glass	el vaso
glasses	los lentes
glove	el guante
goat	la cabra
good	bueno/buena*
gorilla	el gorila
grandfather	el abuelo
grandmother	la abuela
grandparents	los abuelos
grape	la uva
grass	la hierba
green	verde
grey	gris
guitar	la guitarra

Hh

hair	el pelo
hairbrush	el cepillo
hairdresser	el peluquero/la peluquera*
hamburger	la hamburguesa
hammer	el martillo
hand	la mano
happy	feliz
happy birthday!	¡feliz cumpleaños!
hat	el sombrero
head	la cabeza
heart	el corazón
heavy	pesado/pesada*
helicopter	el helicóptero
hen	la gallina
high	alto/alta*
hill	el cerro
hippopotamus	el hipopótamo
hook	el gancho
horn	el cuerno
horse	el caballo
hospital	el hospital
hot	caliente
house	la casa
humming bird	el colibrí
hurricane	el huracán
husband	el esposo

Ii

ice	el hielo
ice-cream	el helado
ice cube	el cubito de hielo
igloo	el iglú

iguana	la iguana
ill	enfermo/enferma*
in	en
in front of	delante de
insect	el insecto
inside	adentro
iron	la plancha
island	la isla

Jj

jacket	la chaqueta
jam	la mermelada
January	enero
jar	el bote
jeans	los vaqueros
jeep	el jeep
jellyfish	la medusa
jewel	la joya
jug	la jarra
juice	el jugo
July	julio
jump, to	saltar
June	junio
jungle	la selva

Kk

kangaroo	el canguro
kennel	la caseta del perro
kettle	la pava; la tetera
key	la llave
kilo	el kilo
kilometre	el kilómetro
king	el rey
kitchen	la cocina
kite	la cometa; el papalote (MEX)
kitten	el gatito
knee	la rodilla
knife	el cuchillo
knot	el nudo

Ll

lace	el cordón
ladder	la escalera
lake	el lago
lamb	el cordero
lamp	la lámpara
leaf	la hoja
leg	la pierna

lemonade	la limonada	mountain	la montaña	paintbox	la caja de acuarelas
lesson	la clase	mouse	el ratón	paintbrush	el pincel
letter	la carta	moustache	el bigote	palm tree	la palmera
lettuce	la lechuga	mouth	la boca	pan	la cacerola
library	la biblioteca	mud	el barro	pancake	el panqueque; la crepa (Méx)
light (daylight, electric light)	la luz	**Nn**		panda	el panda
light (not heavy)	ligero/ligera*	nail	el clavo	paper	el papel
lightning	el relámpago	neck	el cuello	parachute	el paracaídas
lime	el limón	necklace	el collar	parents	los padres
line	la línea	needle	la aguja	park	el parque
lion	el león	nest	el nido	parrot	el perico
lips	los labios	newspaper	el periódico	passenger	el pasajero/la pasajera*
list	la lista	newspaper stand	el kiosco		
listen, to	escuchar	next to	al lado de	passport	el pasaporte
living room	la sala	night	la noche	path	la senda
lizard	la lagartija	nightdress	el camisón	pavement	la acera
lobster	la langosta	nose	la nariz	pawpaw	la papaya; la lechosa (RD, Venz)
lunch	el almuerzo	notebook	el cuaderno		
		noticeboard	el tablero de anuncios		
Mm				peacock	el pavo real
macaw	el guacamayo	November	noviembre	peanuts	los maníes; los cacahuetes (Méx)
machine	la máquina	nurse	el enfermero/la enfermera*		
magazine	la revista				
magician	el mago/la maga*	**Oo**		pear	la pera
magnet	el imán	oar	el remo	pedal	el pedal
main road	la carretera	ocean	el océano	pelican	el pelícano
man	el hombre	October	octubre	pencil	el lápiz
mango	el mango	octopus	el pulpo	pencil sharpener	el sacapuntas
March	marzo	office	la oficina	penguin	el pingüino
market	el mercado	old	viejo/vieja*	people	la gente
mask	la mascarilla	old man	el viejo	pepper (ground)	la pimienta
match	el fósforo; el cerillo (Méx)	old woman	la vieja	person	una persona
mathematics	las matemáticas	omelette	la tortilla de huevos	photo	la foto
		on	en; sobre	piano	el piano
mattress	el colchón	on top of	encima de	picture	el cuadro
May	mayo	onion	la cebolla	pig	el cerdo
meat	la carne	open	abierto/abierta*	pillow	la almohada
medicine	la medicina	open, to	abrir	pilot	el/la piloto*
metre	el metro	orange (colour)	naranja	pin	el alfiler
milk	la leche	orange (fruit)	la naranja	pineapple	la piña
mirror	el espejo	ostrich	el avestruz	pink	rosado/rosada*
Monday	lunes	outside	afuera	pizza	la pizza
money	el dinero	oven	el horno	plane	el avión
monkey	el mono	over	encima de	planet	el planeta
moon	la luna	(go) over	por encima de	plant	la mata
morning	la mañana			plantain	el plátano grande (Méx); el plátano macho (Méx); el plátano (Venz)
mosque	la mezquita	**Pp**			
mosquito	el zancudo	packet	el paquete		
mother	la madre	page	la página		
motorcycle	la moto	paint	la pintura		

plate	el plato	rope	la cuerda	sink	el lavaplatos
play time	el recreo	round	redondo/	sister	la hermana
pocket	el bolsillo		redonda*	skirt	la falda
policeman	el policía	rug	el tapete	sky	el cielo
policewoman	la mujer policía	ruler	la regla	sleep	dormir
pond	el estanque	run, to	correr	slice	el trozo
pool	la charca	runway	la pista de	small	pequeño/
popcorn	las palomitas		aterrizaje		pequeña*
	de maíz				
postman/woman	el cartero/la			smile, to	sonreír
	cartera*			smoke	el humo
post office	el correo	**Ss**		snail	el caracol
potato	la papa	sad	triste	snake	la víbora
present	el regalo	sailboat	el barco de	snow	la nieve
pupil	el alumno/la		vela	soap	el jabón
	alumna*	salad	la ensalada	socks	las medias
puppet	el títere	salt	la sal	sofa	el sofá
puppy	el cachorro	sand	la arena	son	el hijo
purple	morado/	sandwich	el sándwich	soup	la sopa
	morada*	Saturday	sábado	space	el espacio
purse	el monedero	saucer	el platillo	spaceship	la nave
puzzle	el	sausage	la salchicha		espacial
	rompecabezas	scarf	la bufanda	spade	la pala
pyjamas	la piyama	school	la escuela	spaghetti	los espaguetis
pyramid	la pirámide	schoolbag	la cartera	spider	la araña
		scientist	el científico/la	spoon	la cuchara
			científica*	square	el cuadrado
Qq		scissors	las tijeras	stables	la cuadra
queen	la reina	sea	el mar	stairs	la escalera
		seal	la foca	stamp	la estampilla
		seat	el asiento	stand, to	estar de pie
Rr		secondary school	el colegio	star	la estrella
rabbit	el conejo	secretary	el secretario/la	starfish	la estrella de
racket	la raqueta		secretaria*		mar
radio	el radio			station	la estación
rain	la lluvia	September	septiembre	street	la calle
rainbow	el arco iris	shade	la sombra	string	el cordel
read, to	leer	shadow	la sombra	strong	fuerte
red	rojo/roja	shampoo	el champú	submarine	el submarino
reindeer	los rénderes, las	shark	el tiburón	sugar	el azúcar
	caretas	sheep	la oveja	sugar cane	la caña de
	(Venz)	sheet	la sábana		azúcar
		sheet of paper	la hoja		
refrigerator	la nevera	shelf	el estante	suitcase	la maleta
restaurant	el restaurante	shell	la concha	sun	el sol
rhinoceros	el rinoceronte	ship	el buque	Sunday	domingo
rice	el arroz	shirt	la camisa	sunglasses	los lentes de
ring	el anillo	shoes	los zapatos		sol
river	el río	shop	la tienda	sunshade	la sombrilla
robot	el robot	shorts	el short	suntan oil	el bronceador
rocket	el cohete	shoulder	el hombro	supermarket	el
rocks	las rocas	shower	la ducha		supermercado
roof	el techo	sign (notice)	el letrero	swim, to	nadar
room	la habitación	sign (signal)	la señal	swimming pool	la piscina; la
		singer	el/la cantante*		alberca (Méx)

swimming trunks	el traje de baño	tractor	el tractor	whale	la ballena
swimsuit	el traje de baño	traffic	el tráfico	wheel	la rueda
sword	la espada	traffic lights	el semáforo	white	blanco/blanca*
		train	el tren	wife	la esposa
		trainers	los tenis	wind	el viento
Tt		tree	el árbol	window	la ventana
table	la mesa	tree trunk	el tronco	windsurfing	el windsurf
tail	el rabo	triangle	el triángulo	wolf	el lobo
tall	alto/alta*	trolley	el carrito	woman	la mujer
tap	la llave	trousers	los pantalones	worm	el gusano
taxi	el taxi	truck	el camión	write, to	escribir
tea	el té	trumpet	la trompeta		
teacher	el profesor/la profesora*	trunk (elephant's)	la trompa	**X**	
		T-shirt	la camiseta; la franela (Venz)	X-ray	la radiografía
tea spoon	la cucharita			xylophone	el xilófono
tea towel	el paño	Tuesday	martes		
teddy bear	el osito de peluche	twins	los gemelos/ las gemelas*	**Y**	
teeth	los dientes			yam	el ñame
telephone	el teléfono			yellow	amarillo/ amarilla*
television	el televisor	**Uu**			
temple	el templo	umbrella	el paraguas	yolk (of egg)	la yema
tennis	el tenis	(go) under	por debajo de	young	joven
tent	la tienda de campaña	underneath	debajo de	young woman	la chica
		up	hacia arriba	yo-yo	el yo-yo
thin	flaco/flaca*				
throw, to	lanzar	**Vv**		**Zz**	
thumb	el pulgar	vacuum cleaner	la aspiradora	zebra	la cebra
Thursday	jueves	van	la camioneta	zero	cero
ticket	el tique	vase	el florero	zoo	el zoo
tie	la corbata	vegetables	los vegetales		
tiger	el tigre	vet	el veterinario/ la veterinaria*		
toast	las tostadas				
toe	el dedo del pie	video (recorder and tape)	el video		
tomato	el tomate	violin	el violín		
tongue	la lengua	volcano	el volcán		
tools	las herramientas				
toothache	el dolor de muelas	**Ww**			
toothbrush	el cepillo de dientes	walk, to	caminar		
		walking stick	el bastón		
toothpaste	la pasta de dientes	walkman	el walkman		
		wall (inside house)	la pared		
tortoise	la tortuga	wall (outside of house)	el muro		
tourist	el/la turista*	wash basin	el lavamanos		
towel	la toalla	wastepaper basket	la papelera		
tower	la torre	watch	el reloj		
town	la población	water	el agua [F]		
toys	los juguetes	water melon	la sandía		
tracksuit	el equipo de deportes; los pants (Méx)	wave goodbye, to	decir adiós con la mano		
		weak	débil		
		Wednesday	miércoles		

Notes and solutions

Some words have important regional variations. These variations are indicated by (Méx) for words used in Mexico, (Venz) for Venezuela, (PtRi) for Puerto Rico, (RD) for the Dominican Republic, and (Cuba) for Cuba. For example, 'banana' is *la banana*, *el cambur* (Venz), *el guineo* (PtRi), *el plátano* (Méx), where the Spanish *la banana* is the general word and the other three are regional variations.

An asterisk follows words which have a different form in the masculine and feminine. For example, *el aeromozo/la aeromoza* * and *alto/alta**. The symbol [Γ] refers to a feminine word that is used with *el* or *un*, e.g. *el agua*.

Solutions to 'Search forms!' page (page 7)

1a), **2**c) (*el, la, los, las*), **3**b), **4**b), **5**c), **6**b) and c), **7**a), **8**b), **9**c), **10**a) or c)

Look back at this page if you need help finding other words!

Solutions to **Los trabajos** theme page (page 86).

1 el aeromozo	6 la cantante	11 el mago	16 la profesora
2 la artista	7 el chofer	12 la médica	17 la secretaria
3 el astronauta	8 la científica	13 la peluquera	18 el veterinario
4 la bailarina	9 la dentista	14 el piloto	
5 el bombero	10 el granjero	15 el policía	

First published 1999 by
MACMILLAN EDUCATION LTD
London and Oxford
Companies and representatives throughout the world

ISBN 0–333–74728–3

10   9   8   7   6   5   4   3   2   1
08   07   06   05   04   03   02   01   00   99

This book is printed on paper suitable for recycling and
made from fully managed and sustained forest sources.

Typeset by ₮ Tek-Art, Croydon, Surrey
Printed in Hong Kong

A catalogue record for this book is available from the
British Library.

Illustrations by Maggie Downer
Map illustration by Hardlines
Cover illustration by Maggie Downer

Acknowledgements
The publisher would like to thank Hilary Gooden of the Ministry of Education in Jamaica who
first suggested this dictionary.
Also thanks to the advisors Jeannette Allsopp, Aïda Greaves, Juana Toribio de Wynter and Ingrid
Morales de Hernández.